Twayne's English Authors Series

Sylvia E. Bowman, *Editor*

INDIANA UNIVERSITY

May Sinclair

TEAS 192

May Sinclair

MAY SINCLAIR

By HRISEY DIMITRAKIS ZEGGER

TWAYNE PUBLISHERS
A DIVISION OF G. K. HALL & CO., BOSTON

Library of Congress Cataloging in Publication Data

Zegger, Hrisey D
    May Sinclair.

    (Twayne's English authors series ; TEAS 192)
    Bibliography: p. 165 - 72.
    Includes index.
    1. Sinclair, May — Criticism and interpretation.
PR6037.I73Z9   823'.9'12   76-18853
ISBN 0-8057-6666-9

To my mother
and to the memory of my father

Contents

About the Author

Hrisey Dimitrakis Zegger attended Hunter College, received an M.A. in philosophy from the University of Chicago and a Ph.D. in English literature from New York University. She has taught at the State University of New York at New Paltz and at Northeastern Illinois University.

Preface

In the years between 1910 and 1920, before the emergence of Virginia Woolf as a major writer, May Sinclair was considered England's foremost woman novelist. Critics compared her novels to those of the best women writers of the past, most often to those of Charlotte Brontë.[1] Although her reputation since that time has been almost totally eclipsed, a few critics have continued to write favorably about her work. In 1934, Frank Swinnerton wrote that Sinclair "took interesting steps in the novel for which she does not receive full credit."[2] In 1950, Joseph Warren Beach referred to the "firm" and "delicate" quality of her work and wrote that her novels merit additional study and evaluation.[3] In 1967, Walter Allen described her as a "brilliant woman, a fine and at present unjustly neglected novelist."[4]

Since May Sinclair wrote twenty-four novels between 1897 and 1927, as well as two novellas, five volumes of short stories, two of verse, two of philosophy, and numerous essays, it is not surprising that her work is uneven in quality. Instead of giving all her works equal attention, I study in depth in chapters 4, 6, and 7 the three psychological novels on which her importance in literary history and her achievement as a novelist rest. In the introductory chapter on her life and times I briefly touch on her philosophical works and on her poetry criticism.

Sinclair started writing novels in the manner of Mrs. Humphry Ward, novels that were deeply influenced by philosophical idealism dealing with religious ethical questions and spiced with romance and melodrama. She grew dissatisfied with these novels and moved through a second stage of writing realistic, social-problem novels in the manner of H. G. Wells, before she contributed her best work in her psychological novels. Chapters 2 and 3 are devoted to these works.

The aim of this study is to evaluate Sinclair's contribution as a novelist and to place her work in the intellectual and literary movements of her time. Since her work is little known, one of the best ways of achieving this objective is by comparing her work, wherever relevant, to that of the better known novelists of her day. Of all the writers of psychological novels in England, Sinclair belongs most obviously to the age of transition. She was roughly twenty years older than D. H. Lawrence and Virginia Woolf, and we can see in her novels the play of intellectual movements and literary styles that were either assimilated and accepted or outgrown by their time. Sinclair belonged to an earlier generation and shared some of its pieties and methods. Nevertheless, Sinclair's psychological novels, which reflect her knowledge of psychoanalytic writings and her espousal of the theories of the imagist group, are among the early expressions of the modernist tradition in the English novel.

Hrisey Dimitrakis Zegger

Acknowledgments

For permission to quote from May Sinclair's letters I wish to thank Mrs. Muriel M. Sinclair, the widow of Harold Lumley Sinclair, May Sinclair's nephew. I also wish to thank the librarians and staff of the following libraries for making available to me the May Sinclair letters in their collections: Humanities Research Library, University of Texas at Austin; Henry W. and Albert A. Berg Collection, and Macmillan Collection, The New York Public Library, Astor, Lenox and Tilden Foundations; Northwestern University Library; Hardy Memorial Collection, Dorset County Museum; Henry E. Huntington Library; Bertrand Russell Archives, Mills Memorial Library, McMaster University; University of Illinois Library, Urbana-Champaign; Houghton Library, Harvard University; Yale University Library; New York University Library, Division of Special Collections; Bancroft Library, University of California, Berkeley; Brotherton Library, University of Leeds; Manuscripts Division, Library of Congress; University College London Library; Cornell University Library; University of California, Los Angeles, Library; Lockwood Library, State University of New York at Buffalo.

Dame Rebecca West graciously and generously answered my numerous questions about May Sinclair, and Valerie Eliot (Mrs. T. S. Eliot) kindly gave me permission to look at the May Sinclair letters to her husband in the Houghton Library. For their help in my search for the owners of the May Sinclair copyrights, I am indebted to the following: Patrick Singleton Garnett of the law firm Darley, Cumberland and Co.; David Garnett; Curtis Brown Limited; and the Society of Authors. Mr. Peter Weil and the staff of the Newberry Library reproduced the photograph of May Sinclair in the frontispiece, and they provided this and other services with their customary courtesy and efficiency. My husband, Robert Elie Zegger, who has patiently lived with this project for many years, encouraged and helped me at every stage of its progress. Professor Leon Edel read an early version of the manuscript and made helpful suggestions. Lastly, my thanks are due to Professor Dan H. Laurence, who encouraged me to pursue this study and who was generous with his time and with his critical advice.

Chronology

1914   *The Three Sisters; The Return of the Prodigal and Other Stories; The Judgment of Eve and Other Stories.* Moves to house in St. John's Wood. Serves with the Motor Field Ambulance Corps on the Belgian front, from September 25 to October 13.

1915   *A Journal of Impressions in Belgium* and short article "On Imagism."

1916   *Tasker Jevons;* two articles on psychoanalysis, "Symbolism and Sublimation I and II." Elected to Royal Society of Literature.

1917   *The Tree of Heaven; A Defence of Idealism: Some Questions and Conclusions;* a review article on T. S. Eliot, "Prufrock: and Other Observations." Elected to Aristotelian Society.

1918   "The Novels of Dorothy Richardson," an article.

1919   *Mary Olivier: A Life.*

1920 -   *The Romantic; Life and Death of Harriett Frean* serialized
1921   from December, 1920, to March, 1921.

1921   *Mr. Waddington of Wyck.*

1922   *Anne Severn and the Fieldings; The New Idealism.*

1923   Writes *A Cure of Souls.* Publishes *Uncanny Stories.*

1924   *A Cure of Souls; The Dark Night; Arnold Waterlow: A Life.* English delegate to second international P. E. N. Conference in New York City.

1925   *The Rector of Wyck.*

1926   *Far End.*

1927   *The Allinghams; History of Anthony Waring.*

ca. 1929 Incapacitated by illness.

1930   *Tales Told by Simpson,* collection of short stories published singly between 1911 and 1921.

1931   *The Intercessor and Other Stories,* collection of short stories published singly between 1911 and 1923.

ca. 1932 Moves from London to the country in Buckinghamshire.

1946   Dies November 14 in Bierton, Buckinghamshire.

CHAPTER 1

Life and Times

I Early Life

M AY Sinclair, whose full name was Mary Amelia St. Clair
Sinclair, was born on August 24, 1863, in Rock Ferry near
Liverpool of a well-to-do Scottish family.[1] She was the only daughter
and the youngest child in a family of five boys. Her father was a
shipowner in Liverpool, the family business for three generations of
Sinclairs.[2] When she was seven years old her father's business failed,
and her parents separated.[3] May Sinclair lived with her mother in
straitened circumstances, moving about a great deal and relying on
the help of relatives.[4] Although she was usually reticent about her
childhood during interviews and with friends, in her novels she frequently drew upon her early experiences in her family. As May
Sinclair in later life privately acknowledged, *Mary Olivier*, a novel
she wrote in 1919, is almost entirely autobiographical.[5] Indeed,
many similarities exist between the character Mary Olivier and May
Sinclair herself. Although Sinclair adopted the name of May in the
early 1890s, her given name was Mary; Mary Olivier, like May
Sinclair, is the youngest child and only daughter in a family of sons;
and, like May Sinclair, Mary Olivier is born in 1863 and also
becomes a writer.

Sinclair drew on her memories of her own parents and of their
marriage when she portrayed the characters Mr. and Mrs. Olivier,
Mary Olivier's parents.[6] Mr. Olivier, a weak ineffective man, who
secretly drinks to excess, is often at odds with his wife, who is
religious and puritanical. Secure in the knowledge of her own moral
superiority, Mrs. Olivier is the stronger parent and by her show of
quiet suffering controls the family. The Oliviers, who belong to the
Church of England, subject their children to a religious training that
is narrow and repressive. The will of the child is presumed to be

15

wicked and pious conformity is stressed. Mary Olivier is expected to play a role different from that of her brothers: education is stressed for them, but she must confine her interests to household tasks. Mary rebels against her parents' values: despite her mother's misgivings and even ridicule, she reads books from her father's library, teaches herself Greek from her brother's schoolbooks, and writes poetry. From a sympathetic neighbor who belongs to the London Library, Mary borrows books on philosophy. The hard work of reading Immanuel Kant and Hegel provides Mary Olivier with an escape from her boring household tasks; the luminous thought of Plato and Spinoza becomes a refuge from the confused, narrow, and sometimes spiteful religion of her home.

Like Mary Olivier, Sinclair, except for one year at school, was almost entirely self-educated; she, too, trained herself in philosophy about which she eventually wrote two books. In her will, Sinclair bequeathed all her philosophy books to the London Library; she was probably acknowledging her debt to the library for the books which, as she described them in *Mary Olivier*, had been a solace and an escape in her early life.

In addition to her books, Sinclair's childhood pleasures, like Mary Olivier's, included companionship with her brothers, in whose boisterous games she joined and to whom she was deeply attached. At eighteen she was sent to Cheltenham Ladies College, where she had the opportunity to test her powers away from her mother's generally disapproving attitudes. The principal, Dorothea Beale, a formidable Victorian lady not easily given to praise, recognized Sinclair's abilities, encouraged her reading, and published some of Sinclair's philosophical essays in the *Cheltenham Ladies College Magazine*. Her experience at the College must have given Sinclair her first taste of public achievement and recognition. Dorothea Beale tried to steer May Sinclair into religion by way of philosophy, but with Dorothea Beale, too, Sinclair had to wage battles over religious dogma. After a year, Sinclair's mother withdrew her from the school. But Sinclair had gained a window on the world: Dorothea Beale wrote to her, showed her writing to some influential friends, and relayed their praise to her.

With her mother Sinclair continued to live a life of genteel poverty, writing poetry when she could and later earning some money by translating into English a German tome on ecclesiastical history. Her late teens and early twenties and thirties were saddened by the deaths of her father and then of four of her brothers. As the only girl,

Mary Olivier is expected to remain single and to devote her life to running the house for her aging mother; Sinclair also fulfilled this duty by living until early middle age with her ailing mother.

II *Self-abnegation versus Self-development*

May Sinclair remained throughout her life the product of her conventional, pious, and repressive upbringing while, at the same time, she rebelled against it. She was described by her contemporaries as a "shy, remote creature"[7] and as a "quiet, retiring, low-voiced little woman."[8] Dame Rebecca West described her as having "beautiful manners with a Puritan restraint in her bearing. Her voice was notably prim, and her choice of words fastidious."[9] Together with these self-effacing and prim qualities Sinclair also had reserves of grit and courage and a streak of iconoclasm. If the isolation and the battles with her mother in her early life left her outwardly timid, they also left her with an unyielding core, with a tendency to question and challenge authority, and with great sensitivity to any incursions on the freedom and integrity of the individual. She supported publicly some of the progressive causes of her day, such as the suffragist and the psychoanalytic movements, and she did so at a time when psychoanalysis was considered decadent, if not obscene. During World War I, she did such unladylike things as join an ambulance unit and remove the wounded from the battlefields in Belgium. She seemed to have a special penchant for befriending writers who offended middle-class tastes and mores, such as H. G. Wells and Ezra Pound. In addition, she defended a number of times the right of free expression in literature. In 1911 she defended *The English Review*[10] and in 1910 Hermann Sudermann's *The Song of Songs* against charges of obscenity.[11] In 1915, she protested the suppression of D. H. Lawrence's *The Rainbow*.[12]

These two aspects of her nature — self-abnegation and self-restraint on the one hand; iconoclasm, rebellion, and emphasis on individual freedom on the other — are both expressed in her novels. Indeed, the conflict she experienced in her childhood home between denying her will and serving others as against expressing her individuality and developing her potential is central in many of her novels. Though she rebelled against her mother's religion, she retained her moral earnestness, the ideal of self-sacrifice and of service and duty to others.[13] Sinclair substituted for her mother's religion a belief in philosophical idealism as it was developed by T. H. Green, a philosophy that enabled her to reconcile the two sides of her nature. Although the primary ethical category in the philosophy of T. H. Green is the self-realization of man, he also emphasizes the ideals of self-sacrifice and of duty to serve others.

III   *Philosophical Idealism and Influence on her Novels*

T. H. Green's idealism, which had been popularized by Mrs. Humphry Ward's *Robert Elsmere* (1888), was the dominant philosophy of the late Victorian period. Sinclair's introduction to this philosophy came by way of Dorothea Beale. In 1886, when Sinclair was twenty-three years old, she wrote to Miss Beale hinting at a spiritual crisis in which she was losing her faith while finding herself sympathetic to agnosticism. Miss Beale wrote in reply letters of encouragement in which she urged Sinclair to read Green's works.[14]

Dorothea Beale always nurtured the hope that May Sinclair would study philosophy on a formal basis and urged her to go to Oxford and study with Edward Caird.[15] Though she thought well of Sinclair's verse and philosophical essays, she thought writing fiction to be a frivolous, if not disreputable, occupation. When she read Sinclair's first published short story in *Macmillan's Magazine,* she wrote to Sinclair, "I don't consider such things worthy of you. These things are very well as a diversion."[16] Even after Sinclair had published her first novel and had received good reviews, Miss Beale did not surrender her hope of guiding Sinclair back to philosophy. "You must not let yourself be diverted altogether from philosophy," Miss Beale wrote. "Though your philosophy will come out in most things, even in stories, you must give it to us sometimes 'neat.' "[17]

Dorothea Beale's advice to read T. H. Green did not go unheeded. May Sinclair's first published prose work, if one excludes the essays she had written for the *Cheltenham Ladies College Magazine,* was her article of 1893, "The Ethical and Religious Import of Idealism" in which she explicated the philosophy of T. H. Green;[18] Sinclair remained committed to this philosophy all her life. During the war and in the postwar years, by which time the neo-realism of G. E. Moore and Bertrand Russell had replaced idealism as the dominant philosophy at the universities. Sinclair wrote two books defending and explicating philosophical idealism. *A Defence of Idealism* (1917) and *The New Idealism* (1922). The high quality of these books is attested to by the respectful reviews they received in the philosophical journals; for Bertrand Russell wrote favorably of *The New Idealism,*[19] as did R. G. Collingwood.[20]

On the basis of her first book, Sinclair was elected to the Aristotelian Society, a small and select group, in 1917. In the *Proceedings* of the Society, May Sinclair's name appears often as taking part in the discussions that followed the presentation of papers at the monthly meetings. In 1923, she served on the executive committee with five other members, including C. E. M. Joad and A. N. Whitehead.[21] In the same year, at a meeting presided over by Whitehead, she read a paper on "Primary and Secondary Consciousness," a distinction that she felt could successfully meet some of the attacks against idealism.[22] As may be expected from the extent of her interest and commitment to idealism, this philosophy also influenced her novels.

T. H. Green's philosophy was a reinterpretation of German idealism and was formulated in reaction to utilitarianism. In contrast to utilitarianism, which tended to be materialistic, hedonistic, and nonhierarchical, Green regarded man's spiritual nature, his consciousness, as primary; he viewed the universe as being divinely ordered and hierarchical, a manifestation of God's consciousness to which man is related by his own consciousness; and he considered the primary ethical category to be man's self-realization, the need for man and for society to help man reach his best and highest nature. As some of Green's commentators have noted, his language at times is mystical, and his arguments seem to lead to pantheism.[23]

With varying degrees of emphasis, Sinclair expressed many of T. H. Green's ideas in her novels. Concerned about the spiritual, psychological state of her characters, she wrote about their struggles for fulfillment in the midst of adverse circumstances and frustrating human institutions and conventions. She saw the world as divinely ordered, and she regarded man as capable of touching that divinity when he was able to realize his highest self. The ideas with which Sinclair dealt in her novels remain the same, but her emphasis shifted. In her early idealistic novels, she wrote about man's struggle against his environment as a result of which man reaches his highest development and the point at which his life touches a thinly disguised divine power. In the realistic novels, she stressed the social conditions that impede man's self-development. In her psychological novels, she depicted the same struggle for self-realization, but her emphasis is on the mind of the character. In other words, Sinclair first depicted the struggle for self-realization in the formalistic terms of philosophical idealism; she did so, then, in terms of the impeding social environment in her realistic novels; and she finally emphasized the internal aspect of that struggle in her psychological novels.

IV *Philosophical Idealism and Transitional Literature*

The ideas of philosophical idealism, which form the intellectual presuppositions of Sinclair's novels, seem to have also influenced a number of other writers in the transition period; and it seems relevant to place Sinclair's indebtedness to idealism within the wider context of the relationship of this philosophy to transitional literature in general. In different ways, one can trace a connection between idealistic philosophy and the work of H. G. Wells, Henry James, and Dorothy Richardson.

Much of the influence of the philosophy of T. H. Green on his time was toward social reform. For the late Victorian period, his philosophy effectively dealt with the problem of religious doubt by shelving theological issues in favor of good works within society. Instead of emphasizing belief in theological dogma, Green emphasized the virtue of self-development and the responsibility of society to foster it. In this way, T. H. Green substituted for dogma a nontheological humanism. Mrs. Humphry Ward, in her novel *Robert Elsmere*, a best-seller of the nineteenth century, depicted the life of a minister who is so racked by religious doubts that he, on the advice of a philosopher, a thinly disguised depiction of Green himself, gives up his ministry and devotes himself to a life of helping the poor of London. Indeed, as this book's dedication to Green shows, the effect of T. H. Green's philosophy was toward social meliorism. May Sinclair wrote in her article "The Ethical Import of Idealism" that the influence of idealism was beginning to be felt in the "conception of the brotherhood of man that underlies the prominent socialistic ideal."[24]

Sinclair was not alone in her belief that the philosophy of Green had much to do with the rise of the socialistic movement in England. Anne Fremantle in her book, *This Little Band of Prophets*, indicated the similarity between Green's view of the state and that held by H. G. Wells and Beatrice and Sidney Webb.[25] Warren Wagar also noted in a book about Wells that his view of the function of the state was similar to that of the English idealists.[26] Much of the social criticism expressed in the novels of Wells, as well as in Sinclair's realistic novels, was related to the idea of self-realization and to the responsibility of society to foster it that Green's philosophy emphasized.

As Richard Ellmann has stated, the ideal of self-realization is the central theme of transitional literature;[27] Sinclair's concern with this subject clearly had its source in idealistic philosophy. In her early article, she wrote about the idealistic belief in "the right of each individual to the best and the highest that life has to offer him. We regard the individual as under a positive obligation to develop to his utmost all the powers and latent capabilities of his nature."[28] As Ellmann has indicated, this cry for self-realization is central also to the novels of Henry James, E. M. Forster, and H. G. Wells, among others. In James's *The Ambassadors*, Strether's advice is "Live, live, it's a mistake not to"; and, in *The Portrait of a Lady*, Isabel Archer's quest for the full life is also an expression of this ideal. Dorothea Krook has also noted the influence of idealism in James's work.[29] In the work of both James and Sinclair, as in idealistic ethics, the ideal of self-realization goes hand in hand with a strong sense of duty and even of self-sacrifice.

In Dorothy Richardson's *Pilgrimage*, Miriam Henderson's quest is for self-development and self-fulfillment. Miriam sympathetically muses over the ideas of Ralph Waldo Emerson and J. M. E. McTaggart,[30] the Cambridge idealist, she ponders over the problem posed in Mrs. Ward's *Robert Elsmere*;[31] and, in idealist fashion, she finds her happiness in moments of mystical experience, when she has a heightened sense of reality.

V *Philosophical Idealism and the Psychological Novel*

Some of these writers, in whose work the ideal of self-development figured so prominently, were also pioneers in the psychological novel. In general, the idealists, by making consciousness a central metaphysical category, placed new emphasis on this aspect of human nature that had tended to be submerged in the earlier utilitarian theory, as can be seen, for example, in Charles Dickens's characterization of the materialist empiricist Gradgrind in *Hard Times*. In her article about Green, May Sinclair pointed to the importance of consciousness in his philosophy when she described self-consciousness as "the source and ground of reality."[32]

One of the manifestations of this new interest in the human consciousness was the founding in 1883 of the Society for Psychical Research, which included among its members many of the leading idealistic philosophers of the time, such as Henri Bergson, Bernard Bosanquet, F. H. Bradley, and J. H. Muirhead; the latter two had been students of Green.[33] In America, Josiah Royce was a founding member and later a vice-president of the society.[34] Through this organization, the works of Sigmund Freud, Pierre Janet, and Carl Jung were first introduced to England. When the Medico-Psychological Clinic of London, the first clinic to use concepts and techniques of the new psychology in treating mental diseases, was founded in 1913, six of the thirteen founding members, including May Sinclair, were also members of the Society for Psychical Research.[35] The first two Chairmen of the Board of the Clinic, Sir Lawrence Jones and L. T. Hobhouse, were associated with idealistic philosophy. Jones had studied at Balliol[36] where Green had been a Fellow and a Master for about twenty years and where the tradition of his philosophy lived on. L. T. Hobhouse's views on ethics have also been traced to those of Green.[37] Psychoanalysis, with its concern for the development of the individual, was welcomed by those committed to idealistic ethics. Sinclair's interest in the new psychology and her interpretation of it both owed much to her earlier commitment to idealism. For example, she interpreted the psychoanalytic concept of sublimation in terms of Green's concept of self-sacrifice.[38]

With May Sinclair, then, as with some of her contemporaries, a commitment to philosophical idealism led to and supported an interest in social reform and in psychology. Although few specific traces of philosophical idealism appear in her later novels, the influence of this philosophy is much more obtrusive in her earliest novels, such as *The Divine Fire*.

VI *Early Idealistic Novels and Literary Career (1897 - 1906)*

It was not until 1904, when May Sinclair published *The Divine Fire*, that she received public recognition and, in America, acclaim as a novelist. In 1897, when she was thirty-four, May Sinclair had moved to London with her mother;[39] and, from 1897 to 1901, she published two novels and two novellas, all of which received favorable reviews but had modest sales. In contrast to these earlier works, *The Divine Fire* was a best-seller; and Sinclair became overnight the literary success of the year. *The Divine Fire* and *The Cosmopolitan*, a novella published in 1901, are both fictional renderings of philosophical idealism. In an allegorical fashion, they depict the way a man can reach his highest self and the divine through self-sacrifice, through struggling against the evils in his environment, and through service to others. Two earlier volumes of verse that she had published, the first in 1886 when she was twenty-three, had emphasized the same ideals; and one of these volumes had brought a card of praise from William Gladstone,[40] who had helped make Ward's *Robert Elsmere* such a great success through his review in the *Nineteenth Century.*

Sinclair's great success with *The Divine Fire* prompted her literary tour to the United States from mid-November, 1905, to mid-January, 1906, during which she was invited to the White House to meet President Theodore Roosevelt, who admired her novel.[41] During her first few days in America, she received word that her last surviving brother had died suddenly from pneumonia;[42] apparently many of her hosts were unaware of her bereavement. At one of the dinners she attended in New York City, she sat next to Mark Twain, who, exasperated by her shyness, thanked her at the end of the dinner for "a remarkably interesting silence."[43] According to one of her hostesses, "The favorite indoor sport in New York that winter was the effort to draw Miss Sinclair out. No one succeeded."[44] Some of the publicity stunts in connection with her tour, such as invitations to "Divine Fire" parties in the shape of a heart, may have been somewhat embarrassing to May Sinclair; but, once safely back in London, she wrote to an American friend, "I shall always be grateful to America for all it has done for me."[45] In the years after her visit, she sought and was hospitable to visiting American writers, including, in addition to the expatriates Ezra Pound and T. S. Eliot, Robert Frost, Edith Wharton, Ellen Glasgow, Harriet Monroe, and Sinclair Lewis.

VII   Realistic Novels (1907 - 1913)

Sinclair's shyness while she was being lionized because of *The Divine Fire* may have been caused by her doubts about its merits; for some of the critics whose opinions she respected, such as Edward Garnett and Ford Madox Ford, had been less than enthusiastic about this novel. Early in 1905, almost a year before her American tour, she had become critical of *The Divine Fire;* and, in a letter to Edward Garnett, she seemed almost embarrassed by the excessive enthusiasm of some of the novel's admirers in America.[46] Edward Garnett had been critical of Sinclair's *The Cosmopolitan;* and, perhaps with his criticisms in mind while still working on *The Divine Fire,* she began to write a series of novels in which she attempted to implement the canons of realism in her style and in her subject matter. By 1907 in *The Helpmate* and more emphatically by 1913 in *The Combined Maze,* Sinclair had moved to a more realistic, modern phase; for these realistic novels are social-problem novels that are critical of middle-class conventional ideas about women and marriage.

Although these novels were not as popular as *The Divine Fire,*

they received some moderately good reviews; and they helped earn
her the respect and friendship of some of the leading literary figures
of the time. In 1908, she met Thomas Hardy, who said some good
things about one of her lesser novels, and later that year she cycled
with him in the Dorset countryside.[47] In 1912, she met Henry James,
had tea with him, and exchanged observations about the novel.[48] In
the same year, she wrote with obvious pleasure to a friend that James
had come to see her in her flat.[49] Her friends in London, who were
either closer to her own age or about twenty years her junior, were
Ezra Pound, Richard Aldington, Hilda Doolittle (H. D.), as well as
Ford Madox Ford and Violet Hunt. Sinclair had a very high opinion
of Pound and Ford; and, when she took Pound in 1908 to the offices
of the *English Review* to meet Ford, who was then its editor, she
said, according to Ford, that she wanted to introduce "the greatest
poet to the greatest editor in the world."[50]

VIII   *Imagism (1915) and Poetry Criticism*

As early as 1906, Sinclair, in a review-article about three recently
published books of poems by American poets, expressed some disap-
pointment that no American poet had yet attempted to follow the
path created by Walt Whitman: "to escape tradition; to clear the
mind of cant, the cant of iambics; to cast off the tinkling golden
fetters of rhyme."[51] She must have been immediately sympathetic to
the program of the imagists, for their objective was to free poetry
from the traditions of the past. Sinclair's connection with the imagist
group came through her friendship with Ezra Pound, who was put in
charge in 1913 of the literary section of the *New Freewoman*, which
was renamed *The Egoist* the following year.

The imagist number of May, 1915, included a poem by Sinclair
and in the next issue she published an article explicating the principles of imagism. In the years that followed, her sympathetic critical
articles about F. S. Flint, Ezra Pound, H. D., and Richard Aldington
helped to promote the reputation of these emerging poets. Although
Sinclair's comments were favorable in her published articles, she expressed in her private correspondence some reservations about some
of these imagist poets, noting, for example, that the poems of H. D.
and Aldington lacked the strong human passion necessary for great
poetry.[52] If she thought that the achievement of some of the imagists
fell short of greatness, she was in complete agreement with their aim
to revitalize English poetry by replacing the discursive and flaccid
language of much of nineteenth-century verse with a more direct
and intense poetic idiom.

She was also a loyal friend who rallied to their defense when she felt that they were being unfairly attacked by others. In 1920, in an article about Pound in which she tried to turn the tide of public hostility directed against him, she praised his work as a poet and as a critic; she referred to his "incorruptible devotion to his craft"; and she asserted he had done more than "any contemporary critic for the work of Gaudier Brzeska, James Joyce, Wyndham Lewis and T. S. Eliot." She conceded that Pound "may have been guilty of a few blunders, a few indiscretions and impertinences, but he has rendered services to modern international art that in any society less feral than our own would have earned him the gratitude of his contemporaries."[53] She noted with anger that "with one exception every serious and self-respecting magazine is closed to this most serious and self-respecting artist."[54]

Sinclair was ready to praise good poetry in whatever camp she found it. In 1913, she wrote of the "profound vitality"[55] of D. H. Lawrence's poetry; and, in the same year, she exerted herself on Robert Frost's behalf. Frost related that, during his visit to England in 1913, Yeats, Pound, and Sinclair praised his book, *A Boy's Will*, and that Sinclair had been "showing it to people";[56] Frost wrote about Sinclair, "she professes to see something unusual in my book. I like that of course because she is known as an expert in new poetry."[57] Sinclair also helped Charlotte Mary Mew publish her poems and saw to it that her poems were sent to sympathetic critics for reviews.

Not least of the young unknown poets of the time that Sinclair helped with encouraging words and sympathetic appreciation was T. S. Eliot.[58] In 1917, when Eliot was referred to as a "drunken helot" by Arthur Waugh in the *Quarterly Review* and was treated rather offhandedly by the reviewer for *The New Statesman* for his first book of poems, Sinclair wrote an enthusiastic review in which she attacked the reviewer in the *Quarterly* with some witty and barbed comments, defended Eliot's poetry against the reviewer's more rational criticisms, and concluded with an analysis and explication of "Prufrock." She referred to "Prufrock" and to "Portrait of a Lady" as "masterpieces"; and she concluded that, "If there is anything more astounding and more assured than his performance, it is his promise."[59] Indeed, Sinclair's review and Pound's in *The Egoist* were among the very few favorable reviews Eliot's first book of poems had yet received. Although Eliot's book later received favorable comments, Sinclair's remained notable for her perceptiveness.

For example, E. M. Forster and George Orwell both saw "Prufrock" as a refreshingly escapist poem about a bald man in a drawing room; and they thought that Eliot was standing aloof from the problems of the time and was keeping in touch with prewar emotions.[60] To Sinclair, the tragedy of Prufrock is that of "submerged passion"; and Prufrock, "stung by a longing for reality, escapes from respectability into the street." But he realizes too late that "the horrible drawing room life he has entered has got him. His soul can only assert itself in protests and memories. He would have had more chance in the primeval slime."[61] Sinclair also indicated that Eliot's poetry seems obscure because of his trick of "cutting his corners and his curves" and that Prufrock's thoughts "move not by logical stages and majestic roundings of the full literary curves, but as live thoughts . . . move in live brains."[62] In his poetry, Eliot is after reality "stripped naked of all rhetoric, of all ornament."[63] She saw in Eliot's poetry some of the principles of imagism at work; and, by pointing out his method, she made it easier for the reader to understand and to appreciate his poetry.

Pound's statement that Ford Madox Ford, primarily a novelist rather than a poet, was "the critical light" in the years of the imagist movement[64] and Ford's own statement that the imagist poets were practicing what he had prescribed[65] both suggest that a close connection existed between the "new poetry" and the "new novel" at the time. This connection is borne out in May Sinclair's article about the stream-of-consciousness technique in which she applied to the novel some of the principles of imagism. Imagism, with its credo of freedom in the choice of subject matter, of simple and direct language, and of experimentation in technique was one of the literary currents of the era that contributed to the evolution of her novels from their Victorian beginnings to a more modern style and subject matter.

IX Psychological Novels (1914 - 1920)

May Sinclair first read the "new psychology," as the literature of psychoanalysis was then called, at some time around 1913;[66] and this subject seems to have been the single most important influence upon her psychological novels. She tended to assimilate the theories and concepts of psychoanalysis to idealistic ethics, for she regarded psychoanalysis as a means of furthering man's self-development by helping him revolt against, in her own words, "Victorian Puritanism."[67] Under the influence of psychoanalysis, she wrote three of her best novels: *The Three Sisters* (1914), *Mary Olivier* (1919), and *Life and Death of Harriett Frean* (1920). All of these novels are about women who are victimized by their family's demands that they conform to the Victorian ideal of woman as a self-sacrificing, dependent, domestic being who represses her sexual feelings. Although the popular response to these novels was not as favorable as to some of her lesser ones, they elicited favorable comments in literary circles from other writers, such as H. G. Wells, E. M. Forster, and T. S. Eliot.

In 1920, Sinclair was at the height of her powers as a novelist; and she enjoyed the respect of some of the most accomplished writers of her time. In 1922, Eliot wrote to her asking for some of her short stories for *The Criterion;*[68] and, in 1924, she, as well as Bertrand Russell and Rebecca West, was chosen as one of the English delegates to the second international P. E. N. conference in New York. Her house in St. John's Wood,[69] which, according to Rebecca West, was "exquisitely kept,"[70] became a meeting place for some of the young writers of the time; Wyndham Lewis, for example, wrote to Eliot in 1924 that he would deliver his manuscript to Eliot "should you be at May Sinclair's on Thursday."[71]

Although people who did not know her well had thought the younger Sinclair to be aloof and forbidding, she had become with the years less shy and more approachable. Douglas Goldring, for example, wrote that in 1913 he "first met Miss May Sinclair who was then very thin and rather petrifying. I only discovered years later . . . what a really kind and sympathetic woman she was."[72] Another contemporary who knew Sinclair in her mature years observed that "She has real poise, extraordinary grit, and is the most loyal of friends."[73] Others referred to her hospitality and generosity.

X *Final Years as Writer (1921 - 1927)*

In 1921, Sinclair was fifty-eight years old; and, for her, as for other prewar novelists, the world had markedly changed. Her favorite subject matter had been women victimized by society and by the demands upon them of Victorian family life. But by the 1920s — an age of flappers and of habitual debunking of Victorian values — her subject matter had become anachronistic and redundant. When she tried to apply her psychoanalytic point of view to other subjects that did not interest her as deeply, her novels became mechanical illustrations. Indeed, the best work she did in this period were her two novels, *Mr. Waddington of Wyck* (1921) and *A Cure of Souls* (1924), which, though comic, are serious criticisms of English society. By choosing as her protagonists and as the butts of her comic wit a country squire in the first novel and a rector in the second, Sinclair widened her attack on English society to include the values and limitations of the ruling classes.

Perhaps realizing that her writing years were drawing to a close, Sinclair worked at a frenzied pace; for she published, after *A Cure of Souls,* six novels in four years. These novels tend to be repetitive of previous novels and to be thin, sentimental, and melodramatic. However, Sinclair's talent and her critical powers were impaired by her failing health. In the early 1920s, she had developed a slight limp in her walk, the first sign of the neuromuscular deterioration that was to gradually incapacitate her in both mind and body.[74] In the early 1930s, she was moved from her house in London to the country in Buckinghamshire where she died on November 14, 1946.

CHAPTER 2

Idealistic Novels

*T*HE *Divine Fire* and *The Cosmopolitan* are allegorical depictions of the idealistic view of the journey through life. These novels illustrate many of the ethical concepts of philosophical idealism, such as the belief in the necessity for self-development and for self-sacrifice by following universal rather than private ends; a view of evil as the means to the realization of a higher good; and the belief that when man develops his own highest self he realizes the divine in himself.

1 The Divine Fire

The Divine Fire is a study of the development of a poet named Rickman. The first book, "Disjecta Membra Poeta," deals with the early life of Rickman and the impediments in his background and circumstances which he must overcome. He is a cockney whose father, a secondhand bookseller, is concerned only with making money. Rickman works for his father in the dreary atmosphere of the shop, but he finds solace and satisfaction in his books and poetry and in an affair with a cheap actress. In this book, Rickman remains limited by his sexual drives and by the limitations in his background.[1]

In the second book, "Lucia's Way," Rickman experiences a mental and spiritual awakening. When Rickman's father sends him to the Harden estate to catalog the library, at the request of Harden's daughter, Lucia, Rickman is unaware that her father is near bankruptcy. Rickman's father plans to use the cataloging in order to buy the most valuable books cheaply at the bankruptcy sale Rickman spends a number of weeks in the Harden library, and he falls in love with Lucia who, as her name suggests, is the light that awakens Rickman and begins to guide him on his journey to the realization of his own highest nature. Lucia's perfections in beauty,

education, and character, as well as Rickman's feelings of un-
worthiness and awe before her, suggest to the reader that Lucia is a
personification of the divine or the ideal. During the weeks Rickman
spends cataloging the library with Lucia's help, he begins to realize
the shallowness of his relationship with the actress and to be ap-
palled by his father's scheme. When the estate is declared bankrupt,
Rickman confesses to Lucia his father's scheme and, by way of
reparation, refuses to accept payment for his weeks of work at the
Harden library. In short, Rickman has begun a series of self-
sacrifices that mark the way to his moral development.

The third book, "The House of Bondage," records Rickman's suffering as he breaks away from his father and as he tries to live by the
moral conscience that has been awakened by Lucia. Having left his
father's business, he lives in relative poverty in a boardinghouse and
tries to earn his living by writing articles and reviews for literary
magazines. He conceives the idea of buying the Harden library and
presenting it to Lucia in order to make up for the part he had played
in his father's scheme: he begins working very hard and living
frugally, in order to fulfill his objective. This self-sacrifice manifests
his moral development. In the boardinghouse, he meets a pretty
young girl, a clerk looking for a husband, with whom he falls into an
engagement. Although he has escaped the sensuality of his actress,
he is now threatened by the comfortable but suffocating domesticity
that Flossie represents.

In the fourth and final book, "The Man Himself," Rickman
manages to free himself from Flossie, who is happy to be rid of him
when a wealthier suitor appears. Because of his refusal to com-
promise with the tastes of the influential backers of the magazine for
which he writes, he loses his job. Rickman leads a life of great
hardship as he tries to eke out an existence from occasional articles
that he sells to magazines, but he continues writing his own poetry
and saving every penny to buy the Harden library. Through this
period of struggle Rickman is achieving excellence in both his
character and his work. The excellence of his poetry is finally
recognized, and he wins the hand of Lucia. Paralleling the rise of
Rickman is the decline of Jewdwine, a literary critic born with all the
advantages of social position, wealth, and intelligence. At the beginning of the novel, he is engaged to Lucia; but he rejects her when
she loses her money. Gradually, he prostitutes all his abilities
because of his great desire for success and social acceptance

That philosophical idealism provides many of the ideas found in
The Divine Fire can be demonstrated by examining some of the

statements that Sinclair made in her exegesis of Green's ethics. In her article, she stated that moral progress entails "the necessity for self-sacrifice and the obligation to develop self. . . . Only in following selfless and universal ends can man realize his own highest nature."[2] Rickman, who recognizes the obligation for self-development and the necessity for self-sacrifice and self-denial, contrasts with Jewdwine, who only acts to achieve his own success. Also, according to Sinclair's exegesis of ethical idealism, evil "is the necessary means to the realization of a higher good in the perfection of holiness through struggle and temptation."[3] In Rickman's moral progress, he succumbs to and struggles against evil by overcoming the temptations of his father's materialism, the sensuality of his actress, the suffocating domesticity of Flossie, and the literary opportunism of Jewdwine. Sinclair also stated that, "Through more perfect self-sacrifice, man will enlarge the bounds of his personality deepening and broadening into the full life of God."[4] In the novel, this statement is proved true when Rickman's efforts and struggles result in his union with Lucia, which symbolizes Rickman's achievement of his own self and of the divine. Lucia, as her fine character, keen intelligence, and great beauty suggest, is a symbol of the good, the true, and the beautiful.

Ford Madox Ford described the novel as "a fairy tale,"[5] and it certainly is pervaded by an aura of unreality. There are difficulties in trying to make a believable character out of the good, the true, and the beautiful; and Sinclair does not entirely overcome them. In general, the philosophical skeleton of the novel is too obtrusive; and the allegory is at times painfully apparent. For example, Lucia, the means of Rickman's salvation and hence a Christ-figure, is betrayed by her cousin *Jew*dwine; Rickman falls under Lucia's spell when they go for a walk at Easter; on this walk Rickman gets bloody scratches on his hands when he extricates Lucia's skirt from a bramble bush.

The novel also suffers from a tone of high moral elevation that is often strained and from a prose style that is often turgid and rhetorical. Some of the passages reflect a Jamesian concern for the complexities of motives and nuances in relationships between people. These complexities, however, seem to be dictated by a set of ideas imposed by the author; therefore, rather than being subtle or profound, they seem dreary, laborious, and artificial. This novel was, however, the most successful one Sinclair wrote. In the United States, where readers would naturally sympathize with a self-made man who bucked the English class system, the novel sold two-hundred thousand copies.[6] But other reasons for the popularity of *The Divine Fire* on both sides of the Atlantic are not hard to fathom: this most Victorian of her novels ends with the marriage of the protagonist; it shows virtue rewarded and evil punished; and it is written in a prose style that is elevated in tone. Because of the great popularity of this novel, Sinclair was referred to all her life as the author of *The Divine Fire;* ironically, she was primarily known by one of her worse novels.

II   The Cosmopolitan

Another idealistic novel (actually a novella) is *The Cosmopolitan* (1901). The story is about Frida, a young unmarried woman living in the country, whose father expects her to devote her life to taking care of him. Through a visitor to their home, a young painter named Durant with whom she falls in love, Frida glimpses a richer life that she would like for herself. Frida's love for Durant, like Rickman's for Lucia, is the means for her awakening to life's possibilities. Again like Rickman, Frida manages through struggle and self-sacrifice to escape her limited environment and to find fulfillment and even some measure of the divine in her life. The novel ends with her death from a disease she contracted while nursing some poor people in Asia.

In *The Cosmopolitan,* as in *The Divine Fire,* the allegorical aspects are intrusive. For example, Durant is to Frida "a symbol of a reality greater than himself; she loved not him but the world in him . . . it was the lyrical prologue to the great drama of existence."[7] When Durant learns of her death, he muses about the meaning of her life: "She had stretched out her hands to the unexplored, to the unchanged and changing, the many faced, incomprehensible, finite, infinite whole. And she had flung it all up; for what? For a rickshaw coolie's life? Or for something yet beyond?"[8]

May Sinclair's statement that "James has influenced me considerably"[9] is borne out by *The Cosmopolitan* and to a lesser extent by *The Divine Fire.* Both novels center on the development of the protagonists, and this development follows the same pattern F. W. Dupee found in all of Henry James's chief protagonists: "a process of coming into one's own, attaining a sense of identity, through moments of awareness and acts of renunciation."[10] Another Jamesian characteristic found in Sinclair's two novels is a fastidiousness of tone, a preoccupation with what is noble, and a subtly developed moral sense. The protagonists themselves are scrupulous in their conscience and subtle in their analysis of the meaning and effects of their own and other characters' actions. Like many of James's characters, Frida wants to plunge into experience and at the same time has the impulse to renounce it.

The influence of James is most apparent in Sinclair's use of a central intelligence in *The Cosmopolitan;* indeed, the painter Durant, from whose point of view the story unfolds and the characters are portrayed, is like the Jamesian central observer — intelligent, sensitive, sympathetic, and curious. Sinclair referred to Durant in a letter as being "very Henry Jamesy."[11] Frida is revealed through his eyes only gradually by hints and glimpses; and, as he tries to "make Frida out," he engages in considerable speculation about her motives and feelings as well as about those of the characters surrounding her.

Henry James's influence on May Sinclair's early novels was not altogether a fortunate one, since she responded to and emulated one of James's lesser aspects — what one critic has described as James's "bleak world of Higher Perceptions, Noble Ideals, Tender Restraints and Unsung Heroisms."[12] Moreover, James tended to be somewhat veiled and restrained when touching upon such abstract and elevated matters; but Sinclair was unabashedly definite and even allegorical. For example, in *The Wings of the Dove* James surrounded Milly Theale with a veil of tender sentiment; but Sinclair became irksomely allegorical when she described Frida in her death as having "stretched out her hands to the ... incomprehensible, finite, infinite whole."[13] James did not spell out either the meaning of Milly Theale's life or the effects of her death on the relationship of Kate and Densher; but, after her death, their relationship is depicted as a sullied and bitter one. Frida's effect on Durant is described in both very definite and abstract terms; for Durant, a decadent painter, completely changes his art after falling in love with Frida and after her death: "She had shown him the vanity of the sensuous aspect, she had forced him to love the intangible, the unseen. ... The woman lived for him in her divine form, as his imagination had first seen her, as an Idea, an eternal dream. It was as if he could see nothing and paint nothing else."[14] This penchant for the noble and the ideal that May Sinclair shared with Henry James became more a liability in her case because she expressed herself in philosophical and abstract terms. Whereas James emphasized "solidity of specification" and keeping close to reality, in these early novels Sinclair drew characters and actions to illustrate a predetermined set of ideas.

III   *Repudiation of these Novels*

Just a year after the publication of *The Divine Fire* and of *The Cosmopolitan*, Sinclair understood their shortcomings. Of *The Cosmopolitan* she wrote, "Frida is not properly developed and she doesn't convince. I consider *The Cosmopolitan* a failure." In the same letter, she acknowledged her "special vice, a love for too much neatness and completeness of idea. Nature abhors ideas as much as she abhors a vacuum."[15] She seemed almost embarrassed by the success of *The Divine Fire* and ruefully wrote to Edward Garnett, "America continues to enthuse. My last misguided admirer is Prof. Carlton Lewis of Yale. Sad, is it not?"[16]

She was, at least in part, helped in developing her more critical view of these works by two friends, Edward Garnett and Ford Madox Ford. Edward Garnett took her to task for "a priori construction," "lack of reality," and "romancing."[17] In a playful dinner invitation to Garnett, she wrote, "It's been a long time since you sat upon me and poor Ricky in my rooms at Hampstead."[18] Ford Madox Ford was almost brutal in his criticism; when he heard that some people in Boston were giving "Divine Fire dinners" and dressing in some way that suggested the title or characters of the book, he suggested that an appropriate dress would be that of a fireman.[19]

Dissatisfied with these idealistic novels, Sinclair turned in her next few books to realistic methods of writing and to concentrating on social problems. By 1913, she also became dissatisfied with this technique, and once more she took Henry James's work as her model in a series of short stories that she wrote immediately before she began her psychological novels in 1914. Yet even on the basis of these early idealistic novels one can argue that the influence of James was, in certain respects, fruitful in her development as a psychological novelist. In these idealistic novels, as in her psychological ones, Sinclair's chief interest lies in depicting the struggle of the individual to establish his identity through moments of awareness and as a result of moral choices, many of them entailing acts of renunciation. The point has been made that James's use of the central intelligence, according to which the drama unfolds in the mind of the central observer, is the beginning of the stream-of-consciousness technique; for the logical conclusion of this method is to record the activity of the mind itself. Sinclair first used this method in *The Cosmopolitan*, and she carried it to its logical conclusion in a later psychological novel.

Sinclair expressed her admiration for James's works throughout her life, and his was the only literary influence that she acknowledged a number of times in her letters. (One of her prize possessions was a portrait of Henry James by Sargent,[20] which she left in her will to Robert Singleton Garnett, her friend and literary executor.[21]) As she matured in her art, she came to see the importance of James's emphasis on rendering and keeping close to reality; indeed, she was given a vivid lesson about this quality in literature during a social gathering at which James squelched her opinion that the novels of Mrs. Humphry Ward impressed her because of their sense of reality.[22] In 1912, she wrote to Hugh Walpole that she had discussed his *Prelude* with James and had agreed with him that the book is not "close enough to reality" for "your danger lay in a certain vein of fantasy."[23] By 1918, she was criticizing Walpole for the same shortcomings found in her early idealistic novels when she chided him about the "symbolic" and "fantastic" element in his latest book.[24] However, Sinclair did not repudiate the central tenets of the idealistic philosophy that are so readily apparent in her early novels. In her psychological novels her interest continued to center on man's struggle for self-realization and on the rival claims of renunciation, but these ideas are not expressed abstractly but through fully realized experiences. She made the transition to a more vivid way of writing in her realistic novels.

CHAPTER 3

Realistic Novels

*T*HE *Divine Fire* has some passages and incidents that should be considered either realistic or naturalistic. The depiction of Rickman's life of toil and poverty after he leaves his father's business to become a journalist among other compromised and compromising journalists is strongly reminiscent of George Gissing's *New Grub Street*. And the interlude of his illness after he loses his job, when he would have starved but for the help he receives from a neighboring prostitute, is reminiscent of naturalistic French fiction. Jack London and Upton Sinclair were among this novel's most enthusiastic admirers; Jack London wrote to Sinclair that, had he written *The Divine Fire*, he would have been able "to die happily."[1] These two American writers were no doubt drawn by the naturalistic elements in the novel, as well as by the fact that the lowborn Rickman emerges as a moral hero.[2]

In 1897, Sinclair had declared that, "In our modern mythology Custom, Circumstance and Heredity are the Three Fates that weave the web of human life."[3] As she grew older, she began to consider determinism less of a myth and more of a reality in human life. *The Divine Fire*, published in 1904, was an ambitious work that she had begun in 1897, at which time she still viewed the impediments of heredity and environment as obstacles easily overcome; ultimately, they were stepping stones to a higher good.[4] By 1901, her point of view was less optimistic; for with *The Cosmopolitan*, under the combined title *Two Sides of a Question*, she published another novella, *Superseded*, which is decidedly deterministic because it demonstrates how circumstances and heredity can destroy a human being. In *Superseded*, Sinclair depicted another woman, Juliana, who, like Frida in *The Cosmopolitan*, is condemned by her environment to a limited stifling life. Unlike Frida, however, Juliana cannot escape; she has neither the money nor the strength of character and intelligence to create a new life for herself. Although Sinclair never states her intention so simply, these two stories, as their combined title implies, present two sides of the question: idealism and freedom versus naturalism and determinism. In the novels which followed these novellas, the naturalistic point of view seems dominant: circumstance and heredity determine human life.

I Superseded

Juliana Quincey, the protagonist in *Superseded*, is a forty-five-year-old spinster who has taught mathematics for twenty-five years at an upper middle-class school for girls. Although a dull and pedestrian teacher, she works hard and conscientiously at her teaching; and the school has become the center of her life. The new headmistress, who feels that Miss Quincey is too old and not up to the standards of the school, wants to dismiss her. When Miss Quincey becomes ill, she enjoys a brief respite from the head-mistress's scorn; and, under the care of a young doctor, who shows her more attention and sympathy than any man has ever done, her spirits revive and she experiences what amounts to her first and only love affair. But the eighty-year-old aunt with whom Miss Quincey lives notices her infatuation and taunts her back into her usual dispirited self. Ten months after her dismissal from the school, having used up the twenty-six pounds she managed to save during twenty-five years of teaching, Miss Quincey dies; and the young doctor marries the young and beautiful classical mistress he met while attending Miss Quincey.

Superseded fulfills many of the criteria of naturalistic fiction. A materialistic, deterministic philosophy underlies the narrative, for Miss Quincey is fated by heredity and circumstances, by her dullness and by her lack of imagination, good looks, and money. Twice in the course of the story Miss Quincey reaches for spiritual values, and both times these values betray her. Her first illness afflicts her when she has overtaxed her strength by trying to follow the headmistress's injunction to acquire general culture by reading the great poets. The second time that spiritual values betray her occurs when she allows her feelings to thaw somewhat by basking in the sun of the doctor's attention and by falling in love with him. The principle of "survival of the fittest" also seems to be at work; for, as a weak person, she is destined to failure. And, in this respect, Miss Quincey's sister and the classical mistress are contrasts, since both of them are beautiful, intelligent, and have brilliant careers and happy marriages.

In this novella Sinclair made concrete Zola's comparison between
the novelist and the doctor, for Sinclair's young doctor acts as her
surrogate when he presents Miss Quincey's life in deterministic
biological terms by observing that "your race is to the swift and your
battle to the strong."[5] He also believes that the movement for
woman's emancipation that emphasizes education and careers for
women can be destructive if it does not take into account each
woman's abilities and her basic human sexual nature. Having an
education and a career may be liberating for gifted and energetic
women like the classical mistress and Miss Quincey's sister; but, for
an average woman like Miss Quincey, such benefits simply mean
dehumanization as a student and later exploitation as a worker.
Although the classical mistress at first scoffs at the doctor's ideas, she
agrees with him after Miss Quincey's dismissal "that there was a side
to the subject that her friends the idealists were too ideal to see."[6]

Although *Superseded* is naturalistic in many respects, it is not a
"slice of life"; for the narrative is meticulously structured in order to
present in twelve brief chapters the fate of the protagonist. The
novel opens with a scene in which Miss Quincey's being pushed into
a corner by a procession of St. Sidwell's girls causes the headmistress
to look disapprovingly at her awkwardness. The novel ends with a
scene in which the classical mistress and the doctor, now happily
engaged, leave the cemetery where they have just visited Miss
Quincey's grave. Both the procession of girls and the engaged couple
are suggestive of the life, the youth, and the happiness that have
eluded Miss Quincey. In the intervening chapters Miss Quincey's
fate unfolds: she attempts to expand her horizons by reading the
great poets; she undergoes her first reversal when she becomes sick
from overwork; the seed of her subsequent undoing is planted by the
doctor's visits; she falls in love with him, is taunted by her aunt, and
is dismissed from the school; after she observes the love shared by
the classical mistress and the doctor, she recognizes her own futility;
soon after she dies. The plot of the story closely follows the course of
a Greek tragedy; and, although Miss Quincey hardly has the stature
of a tragic heroine, the reader experiences a relentless and swift un-
folding of her destiny.

There are many felicitous touches where a compassionate irony
underscores the pathos of Miss Quincey. When the headmistress in
her inaugural address instructs her staff to read the great poets for
their regenerative and healing powers, Miss Quincey, thoroughly
impressed with, and awed by, this new responsibility, writes in her

notebook "Poets - healers and regenerators."[7] In another passage
Sinclair comments ironically about Miss Quincey's age: "And now
she was five and forty; she had always been five and forty; that is to
say, she had never been young, for to be young you must be happy.
And this was so far an advantage, that when middle age came on her
she felt no difference."[8] Miss Quincey joins a teacher's debating
society where she listens to a speech "on the emancipation of
women; about the women's labor march, about the doors that were
now thrown open to women. She was told that all they wanted was a
fair field and no favour. (The speaker, a rosy-cheeked child of one-
and-twenty, was quite violent in her repudiation of favour.) And
Miss Quincey believed it all, though she understood very little about
it."[9]

No villains are in the novella, for the headmistress, though cold
and ruthless, is trying to improve her school; the doctor acts as he
does because of his sympathy and humanity; and even the old aunt
who tortures Miss Quincey acts from habit, for her niece has become
the scapegoat on which she vents the irritability of her age.
Superseded is one of Sinclair's most successful works, since it conveys in one hundred and twenty-five pages the pitiful story of the old
and rejected — and does so without sentimentality. Her prose is
restrained and objective and lacks the flights into the empyrean that
mar her idealistic novels.

II *Realistic Novels on Marriage*

Most of Sinclair's pre-World War I works were realistic novels of
ideas in which man is shown to be influenced to a large extent by circumstances and heredity. In these novels, she exposed the social conventions and ideas that impede man's self-development. Indeed,
Sinclair seems to have taken Professor Grey's advice to Robert
Elsmere and to have turned her attention from metaphysics to social
reform. Hence there is no contradiction between these realistic
novels and her idealistic philosophy; she was writing according to
that side of Green's philosophy that emphasized social action and
social reform as the best way of serving God and of reaching moral
excellence by helping other men realize their highest natures. The
social problem to which Sinclair directed her attention in these
novels was primarily that of the position of women in society whose
progress was impeded by conventional ideas about women and by
the flaws in the institution of marriage.

Whereas *The Divine Fire,* in the usual Victorian fashion, ends

with the peal of wedding bells, her realistic novels begin with
marriage. The novel of marriage — or more precisely of marital incompatibility — to which genre most of Sinclair's realistic novels
belong was enjoying something of a vogue at the turn of the century;
and its popularity has been attributed variously to the influence of
the French novelists, to Henrik Ibsen, and to the suffragette movement. Although Sinclair's realistic novels show the influence of
naturalism, her final outlook was not deterministic; she used
naturalistic themes to attack Victorian points of view, such as those
of Coventry Patmore and Charles Kingsley, about marriage and
women. These writers tended to emphasize the spiritual aspect of
marriage; Sinclair emphasized its instinctual basis. They viewed
marriage as an elevating and harmonious institution; Sinclair often
pictured it as being destructive. They tended to see the "angel-in-
the-house" type of woman as the ideal mate; Sinclair showed the
devastating effect that type of woman could have on a man.

III   Mr. and Mrs. Nevill Tyson

Sinclair's novel *Mr. and Mrs. Nevill Tyson* (1898) depicts a
marriage both as it really is and as it appears to be. At the opening of
the novel, Mr. Tyson, a rather superficial person with a strong sensual nature, marries a very pretty, vivacious woman who is socially
beneath him. Because of her low origins, her gaiety, and her enjoyment of men's attentions, people consider her to be a flirt and quite
improper. After some time, her husband begins to tire of her; and,
when the difficult birth of a child affects her beauty, Mr. Tyson
begins to reject both his wife and his child. Realizing his jealousy of
the child and not wanting to estrange him further, Mrs. Tyson reluc-
tantly lets the child be looked after by a servant under whose
negligent care the child dies. People condemn her for having
neglected the child, and her husband deserts her.

Under the stress of her suffering, Mrs. Tyson begins to develop
her mind and her soul. She reads a good deal, and she tries to retain
her memories of her husband by being friendly with her husband's
best friend. The village people condemn her, for they believe that
she is having an affair. When her husband catches a glimpse of her
in his friend's company, his jealousy is aroused; and his interest in
her begins to revive. He returns, makes love to her, and vows his
fidelity. That night in an accident while drunk, he sets the house on
fire. In Mrs. Tyson's efforts to save him, she is burned and badly dis-
figured. Mr. Tyson tries to be kind to her; but, because of her dis-

figurement, all his love is gone; and he leaves her to be a soldier in the Sudan. She dies from her burns and from the shock of his desertion, and he is killed while fighting in the Sudan. The village people build a statue of him and extol his heroic deeds, and they regret his having married a common woman unworthy of him.

The view of marriage that emerges is not that of the enobling Victorian institution: it is a confining, bitter bond for Mr. Tyson, who cannot restrain his roving sensual nature; and it is a private hell for Mrs. Tyson, who sacrifices her child in a vain attempt to keep her husband. Beneath the public facade of marital unity, one that is also implied by the title *Mr. and Mrs. Nevill Tyson*, is a world of misunderstanding, frustration, and pain. The imagery of the novel, predominantly that of animals, also serves to undermine the spiritual, idealized view of marriage. Tyson's animal appetites are indicated by his references to his wife as a "mare," a "butterfly," a "bird," and a "little animal"; and to his son as a "rat" and a "pig." In the scene of Mr. Tyson's death in the desert, Sinclair implied the carelessness of nature and its indifference to human suffering and aspirations. Tyson and his men become sick in the inhospitable desert environment; and, after their deaths, the sands of the desert cover their bodies and scatter their tents and their possessions.

In contrast to this naturalistic treatment of Mr. Tyson is the largely idealistic treatment of Mrs. Tyson. She is at first a pretty, foolish young woman; but, as a result of her suffering, as is consonant with Sinclair's interpretation of idealistic philosophy. Mrs. Tyson develops her mind and her soul; and she dies from the burns she receives in her self-sacrificial effort to save her husband's life. However, Sinclair's characterization of Mrs. Tyson is not convincing because her change from a seemingly gay flirt to a noble soul is not entirely believable. Furthermore, the use of both an idealistic and a naturalistic point of view in the same novel results in a lack of cohesion. Indeed, Sinclair's naturalism seems, at best, half-hearted. The deterministic Sudan episode is not quite "earned" in the context of the novel, and it appears to be Sinclair's attempt to give cosmic significance to the events of the novel.

Despite such flaws, the work as a whole has qualities of delicacy, perceptiveness, and intelligence. Mr. Tyson, who is by no means the villain, is depicted as coarse, as a bit of a fool, but as well meaning but weak. The reader finds something rootless and pathetic about him, something fundamentally inept and bungling. Having recently inherited a country estate, he takes great pains to hide his origins in trade. When he enters country politics, he offends the very people it was his intention to please. His final stand in the Sudan, though considered heroic by his village, is depicted as a foolish and tragic gesture which results in the death of all his men.

Most of the events in the novel are presented from the point of view of Mr. Tyson's best friend, who disapproves at first of the apparently light-headed wife of his friend but who gradually begins to love her. By seeing the events from the friend's perspective instead of from an omniscient author's, the reader enjoys the excitement of limited knowledge and tentative evaluation. Although the depiction of Mrs. Tyson does not succeed, other compensations exist in the novel. The intense struggle between the Tyson couple is relieved by scenes of English country life — of gossip, of racing, and of teas with a spinster of intellectual pretensions and a pompous, inane, but kind country squire. These people touch the lives of the two main characters, and they provide a background of normal life for the sometimes melodramatic scenes in the novel. Despite their kindliness, the village people are blinded by their undue regard for the conventions; and, as a result, they unintentionally but cruelly misjudge the two main characters.

IV The Helpmate

May Sinclair's next novel in her series about marriage, *The Helpmate* (1907), continues to undercut Victorian ideals about marriage and women. By 1907, the presence of ideas in a novel seems to have become almost a criterion of excellence; for, as a critic in the *Edinburgh Review* stated that same year, "the appeal of novels lies not so much in the story as in the range of ideas they represent and illustrate." To another critic, "all novels should be contributions to the liberal education of readers."[10] In *The Helpmate*, the characters and the events exist to illustrate an idea that is rather obvious to the reader of the 1970s: the spiritual wife can cause suffering, and marriage without sex is difficult. Perhaps one can only add in defense of Sinclair's novel that in 1907 the view that women are and should be asexual was still rather widely held. Lawrence Jones in his *Edwardian Youth* recalled a group of Oxford undergraduates' asking a doctor whether a woman ever enjoyed sexual intercourse. The answer was, "Nine out of ten women are indifferent to it or actually dislike it; the tenth who enjoys it will always be a harlot."[11]

Anne Majendie, the heroine and the "helpmate," is a woman patterned after the Victorian ideal of woman; for, as Kingsley described her in 1870, the ideal woman is "the teacher, the natural and therefore divine guide, purifier, inspirer of man."[12] Anne discovers during her honeymoon that her husband had had an affair with a woman before he had met her. Although Anne despises him for his weakness, she gradually accepts the situation almost with pleasure; for she regards her marriage as a sacrifice that entails her suffering, "the seal God set on her soul," and that gives her the responsibility of saving her husband by "raising him to her own spiritual state."[13] In short, Anne becomes her husband's moral teacher.

Her husband takes great pains to show that he has repented for his past deed; and, as a result of a temporary reconciliation between them, a child is born. But Anne's standard of spiritual purity is so unnatural that he is finally driven to having an affair with a more comfortable woman. After much suffering, Anne realizes at the end of the book that "her goodness had been her husband's ruin" and the two are reconciled. "She saw that there was no spirituality worthy of the name that had not been proven in the house of the flesh,"[14] but her husband more bluntly explains that "It's as simple as hunger and thirst: and if there's no clean water you drink dirty water."[15]

Sinclair felt strongly antagonistic to the old concept of women as the purifiers of men and as spiritual domestic creatures devoid of sexual drives, and *The Helpmate* was an attempt to undermine that stereotype by showing the marital conflict and unhappiness it could create. She also believed that such a stereotype prevented women from fulfilling themselves as human beings by considering them too pure and too delicate to take part in the world outside the home. She herself experienced the injustice of this stereotype when the Aristotelian Society refused to admit her, and she complained to Bertrand Russell: "They said they would not have women in because you can't knock them about. Now I don't mind being knocked about; in fact, I like it."[16] At this time, she was so actively engaged in the suffragist movement that, as Violet Hunt has related, she and May Sinclair spent three days in the High Street Station with wooden boxes collecting money for the movement.[17] In an article on George Meredith, Sinclair wrote appreciatively of his "large-hearted" and "large-brained" women; and she remarked that "He was the first to see that the sentimentalism of his time was a degradation to its women."[18] In the pamphlet "Feminism," Sinclair argued for giving women a wider scope; and she quoted George Bernard Shaw's words from *Getting Married*, "such a born wife and mother all the children ran away."[19]

Unfortunately, Sinclair's message was more important to her than

her art, for the novel is, on the whole, wooden. Anne and her husband are pale shadows, and the novel has many melodramatic
scenes. Nonetheless, the reviewer in the *Times Literary Supplement*,
whose critics had written some unfavorable comments about some of
Sinclair's better novels, regarded this one favorably as a "fine,
sincere, and fearless" novel; moreover, "its courage and understanding raises its author to a place very little below the first rank of
living novelists."[20] To Ford Madox Ford, who wrote a more perceptive review, the novel was flawed by being too much a study of a
problem; but, at the same time, he regarded it as an advance over
The Divine Fire because it was "down in the ground and possible":
"There's more beef in it and it deals with a real problem of life."[21]
Although *The Helpmate* seemed in its own day to be a "courageous"
and "outspoken" novel — so much so that the American Library
Association required it to be stored on the restricted shelf — the
novel can only be considered a historical curiosity today.

V   The Judgment of Eve

In *The Judgment of Eve*, a novella first published in 1907, May
Sinclair managed to control her didactic tendencies so effectively
that one reviewer complained that the moral of the tale was not
clear. To Sinclair, *The Judgment of Eve* was an experiment in compression, and she shows in one hundred and twenty-two pages the
gradual disillusionment with, and deterioration in, a marriage that
lasts for seven years. Aggie, the "Eve" of the title, is an idealistic
young woman who turns down a prosperous farmer from her village
to marry a clerk in a solicitor's office in London, a man who seems
more refined and who shares her interests in music, art, and poetry.
During the first year of their marriage, they go to lectures and
museums in London; and both feel happy and superior to couples
with more worldly goods but with fewer cultural interests. But, after
the children start arriving, one every year, their trying to provide
and care for them erodes all their pretentions to culture; and their
life becomes harried and mean. The husband, overworked and anxious about money, is increasingly short-tempered and resentful of
the children. Although the doctor warns him that another pregnancy
would kill Aggie — a conversation she overhears — he is too self-
involved and too petulant to abstain from sex or to take precautions.
The seventh pregnancy does indeed kill Aggie; but, before she dies,
she tells her family that it was she who had wanted to keep having

children; for she hopes thereby to shield her husband from their anger.

As in Sinclair's previous realistic novels, she seems to be weighing against each other a deterministic and an idealistic view of life. This story of marriage becomes one about the gradual undermining of ideals and spiritual values by poverty and sex. Aggie, by choosing Arthur Gatty over the prosperous farmer, John Hurst, was trying to evade and transcend nature since she preferred Arthur Gatty only because he seemed more refined. Years later, after seeing what a kind husband John Hurst proved to be for her sister, Aggie realizes that "her little undeveloped soul, with its flutterings and strugglings after the immaterial, had been repelled by the large presence of the natural man."[22] In choosing Mr. Gatty instead of Mr. Hurst, spirit over nature, she had tried to defy nature; but nature takes vengeance on this slight.

Sinclair described this story as a tale of retribution, and the word "judgment" in the title refers both to Aggie's judgment in choosing Mr. Gatty and also to nature's judgment on Aggie. By referring to Aggie as Eve in the title, Sinclair is perhaps suggesting that the plight of Aggie, who seeks in marriage more values than are part of nature's plan, is the plight of every woman. Yet the victory is Aggie's, for her love for her husband, which is underscored by her lie to her family, has survived. In the final pages, Sinclair refers to Aggie's "incorruptible love and divine tenderness."[23]

Today's reader may recoil from such situations and statements and may not only find Aggie, whose name Agatha suggests the Greek word for "good," too much of a submissive, patient Griselda type but also think the novella itself too sentimental. Yet, in comparison to *The Helpmate*, Sinclair, on the whole, has much more artfully controlled her didactic tendencies. The conflict between nature and spirit that underlies the story is either concretely rendered or, in most places, suggested subtly enough to prevent the ideas from overwhelming the story. For example, the account in the opening pages about Aggie's feelings toward her two suitors — one in which Aggie's conflict is suggested — is done with grace, delicacy, and humor:

Though she wouldn't have owned it she had been attracted by John's [the farmer's] appearance. Glancing out the drawing-room window she could see what a gentleman he looked as he crossed the market-place in his tweed suit.

cloth cap and leather garters. He always had the right clothes. When high collars were in fashion he wore them high. His rivals said that this superstitious reverence for fashion suggested a revulsion from a past of prehistoric savagery. Mr. Gatty, on the other hand, had a soul that was higher than any collar. That, Aggie maintained, was why he always wore the wrong sort.[24]

The deterioration of the Gatty seven-year marriage is vividly and economically evoked by the use of a number of details. When the couple first furnish their house, they buy copies of three pictures by Burne-Jones, "Hope," "Love Leading Life," and "Love Triumphant"; and, as their marriage deteriorates, the pictures become a reminder of their perishing dreams. When the first baby comes, Aggie sings a nursery rhyme that is also the epigraph of the story: "I saw a ship-a-sailing, a-sailing on the sea/And it was full of pretty things for Baby and for me." The nursery rhyme keeps recurring in the story, a leitmotiv that again emphasizes the frustration of their hopes.

In the contrast between the two sisters — Susie, who marries the natural man, and Aggie, who marries the more intellectual man — Sinclair first touched on a theme that recurs in her psychological novels; for central to each one of them is a woman who tries to defy nature and suffers as a result. In all her works up to this time, with the exception of *The Divine Fire*, Sinclair was exploring the subject of the nature of woman; and her point of view was a complex one. On the one hand, she rejected in *The Helpmate* the Victorian conception of woman as an asexual, morally superior being. In Susie she drew the opposite of Anne in *The Helpmate*, for Susie is the natural woman who is led by her instincts and is happy as a result. However, in Aggie Sinclair draws the first of her many portraits of women who are sexually responsive but who feel a conflict between their natural instincts and their ideas or spiritual expectations and suffer as a result. (Perhaps Sinclair was reflecting the historical record when she viewed women who sought to fulfill both their instinctual drives and their intellectual aspirations as doomed to suffer.) D. H. Lawrence, who was later concerned with the same subject of sexual fulfillment, also viewed the woman led by her instincts to be the healthiest. However, he disliked the type of woman who feels a conflict between nature and spirit, for he viewed such women characters both as nuisances for their male partners and as victims of a neurosis. Nevertheless, in his male characters, like Paul Morel, he viewed the same conflicts sympathetically.

VI Kitty Tailleur *and* The Creators

George Bernard Shaw's *Man and Superman,* which was performed for the first time in 1905, created a great stir and opened a public debate about woman's nature; for, in his play, he reversed the Victorian concept of woman as a spiritual, asexual being by portraying Ann Whitefield's essential nature as sexual and as the procreative function for the Life Force. May Sinclair entered the fray when she published in the book section of the *New York Times* a humorous article in the form of a conversation which occurs at a luncheon party in which each person has a different point of view about the character of Ann Whitefield. "The physiologist," who thoroughly approves, believes that every faculty in a woman is subordinated to her physiological functions; the "educational lady" believes that, while women should be educated first to be good wives and mothers, for them to act as if the whole universe is merely a matrimonial bureau is unseemly; the "sentimental lady" is offended because Shaw overlooks the soul. The "student of human nature," through whom Sinclair herself speaks, tries to mediate between all these different views. She agrees with the physiologist that maternal instincts may be the root of a woman's life, but she insists that the role of woman is more than procreative. Life entails the perpetuation not only of the race but of a civilization; and to contribute to and transmit a civilization is the function not only of man but of woman also. Shaw, according to the student of human nature, "ignores the super-woman";[25] but, after the student observes that the hostess, who is devoted to her loutish son and dull husband, is a very happy woman, she concludes that the maternal instincts may, indeed, rule a woman's life.

Sinclair was as much concerned with showing that woman was more than just a sexual reproductive being as she was in burying the Victorian stereotype of woman as an asexual "angel in the house." In *Kitty Tailleur* (1908) she made her protagonist a demimondaine and showed that even such a woman could rise above her physical nature. In *The Creators* (1910), she dealt with the life of a "superwoman," a woman author who tries to fulfill both her sexual maternal instincts and her desire to write. Though enlightened and humane in their views on women, these two novels are among May Sinclair's poorest.

In *Kitty Tailleur,* or in the American edition titled *The Immortal Moment,* a respectable widower with two young daughters falls in love with Kitty during his holiday at a hotel. She loves him, she is tempted to accept his proposal of marriage, but she finally decides to tell him about her past because she is afraid that she may unconsciously corrupt his two daughters. Her "immortal moment" becomes her renunciation of happiness; for, as she tells a character in the novel, "I've only been good for one moment. One moment when I gave Robert up. Do you think it'll count?" Her listener replies, "In the eyes of God, such moments last forever."[26]

In 1907, Lady Robert Cecil, the wife of one of England's most prominent Tory peers, wrote an article that condemned *The Helpmate* for preaching a doctrine of "spiritual redemption by way of fleshly sin"[27] and that also decried the fact that "all the technically impure people are presented as saints."[28] Sinclair was perhaps rebutting Lady Robert's assumption that respectability and moral worth are the same when she portrayed Kitty as a moral heroine who tells her wooer about her past and who willingly sacrifices her happiness. Although Kitty would like to lead a conventional moral life, "respectable" people make it almost impossible; for she cannot sit in the hotel lounge by herself without being bothered by the men's making advances and the ladies' ignoring her but gossiping maliciously about her. For a youthful indiscretion Kitty's parents barred her from their home and thereby sacrificed their daughter to their notions of propriety. Kitty is portrayed as a victim of man's cruelty and lechery, but, by her own moral courage and self-sacrifice, she redeems herself.

In many respects Kitty is a creature of fantasy, for her life as a demimondaine seems not to have affected her character at all. Like a heroine in a Henry James novel, she is prone to making the most discriminating moral distinctions; and, since Sinclair includes very little that is naturalistic in this novel, the instincts and the circumstances that have shaped Kitty are barely suggested. There are, however, indications that Sinclair was experimenting in this novel with a subjective Jamesian method; for, in the earlier part of the novel, the reader's interest lies in trying to put together a coherent view of Kitty, who is presented through the eyes of four different people, each of whom sees her differently; and much of the latter part of the novel is devoted to Kitty's ruminations as she tries to decide whether to tell Robert about her past. However, Sinclair was trying to write not only a Jamesian novel but also a social tract that countered both traditional social views and "revolutionary" Shavian ideas that women are ruled by their instincts. Partly because her aims were so diverse, the novel is an uneven mishmash. Nonetheless, Thomas Hardy made some favorable comments about this novel; but he may have done so because of his friendship with Sinclair or because he admired her courage in portraying Kitty as a "pure woman" when she was, technically speaking, less pure than his Tess.[29] In 1891, when *Tess of the d'Urbevilles* was published, Hardy was vilified for referring in his subtitle to adulterous Tess as a "pure woman."

In *The Creators, A Comedy*, Sinclair deals with the difficulties women writers have in trying to fulfill their sexual and maternal instincts and do their creative work. The protagonist, Jane Holland, is a successful writer who marries an editor and who finds being a wife, a mother, and a writer fraught with conflict. Though her future husband and his family admire her talent and her success when he is courting her, they later consider her interest in writing as a threat to the happiness of the family and as somehow neurotic. Jane makes a heroic and exhausting effort to complete one novel; but her husband, feeling neglected during this interval, nearly falls in love with his secretary, a woman who lives for his comfort and who tries to anticipate and meet his every need and mood. At the end of *The Creators*, Jane's husband loyally defends his wife against his family's criticisms; but the reader is left with the impression that Jane has found the struggle so exhausting she will give up her writing.

Two other women writers in the novel act as foils for Jane. One experiences no conflicts, for her husband, a poet named Prothero, is thoroughly unworldly and feels no resentment about his wife's writing. Unlike Jane she has no desire to have children. The second woman writer, Nina, is spared Jane's conflict because she is such a passionate, fierce woman that men find her overwhelming and keep their distance. She is lonely and suffers; but since her artistic gifts appear to flower under these conditions, Sinclair seems to imply that most women writers, if they wish to make the most of their gifts, must share Nina's fate. In contrast to these three women is a male writer, Tanquery, whose life is the easiest of all; for, in a rather casual way, he marries a sweet self-effacing girl who had been his servant. She makes absolutely no demands on him, and he easily ignores and neglects her while he devotes himself to his art.[30] However, the world at large sees nothing wrong with Tanquery's treating his wife as a domestic convenience; and he feels no guilt and has no conflict about neglecting her.

This novel is one of Sinclair's least attractive ones because, in writing about "creators," she lapses into some of the fervid hyperbolic prose with which she had written about the same subject in *The Divine Fire*. She became seriously ill when she was working on this novel; but, because the novel was being serialized while she was working on it, she had to meet publication deadlines. Much of the prose is limp and careless; and, when her imagination flagged, she tried to compensate by overwriting. Moreover, the novel lacks an organic unity; for, although the subtitle *A Comedy* indicates that Sinclair intended to write one, the material took another shape, and she could not rewrite what had already appeared in print. In addition, the editor kept making alterations and deletions to avoid offending the reader, thereby further blurring the focus of the novel. Although some comedy exists in Tanquery's wooing of Rose, the novel is singularly lacking in humor. In fact, the "creators" always talk about their own and each other's works with portentious seriousness. The novel ends with the death of the unrecognized poet Prothero and with Jane's exhaustion and thoughts of giving up her writing.

In *Kitty Tailleur* and in *The Creators*, Sinclair was trying to develop a fiction that was different from her previous realistic novels of ideas. In *Kitty Tailleur*, she experimented with a more subjective technique; and *The Creators* was to be, as she had written to the editor, "a novel of character" rather than of social problems — one that was to show the way in which the creative drive affected different people.[31] Indeed, she planned for *The Creators* to be a major novel, a second and better *Divine Fire*.[32] By the time she completed it, she was so thoroughly dissatisfied with the results that she confided to a friend that she grew to "hate it."[33] In her next novel, she returned once again to the realistic novel of ideas.

VII   The Combined Maze

Although *The Combined Maze* (1913) is like her previous realistic novels of ideas in technique and subject matter, the novel marks an advance in her prose style. In 1910, she wrote to Ford Madox Ford that she admired his compression, a skill in writing that she felt she often lacked.[34] By 1912, she had also become a good friend of H. G. Wells; and, with the examples of Wells and Ford to follow, she made her prose sparer, easier, and more conversational. There is no trace in this novel of the florid prose that marred some of her previous novels nor of the epigrammatic, balanced sentence structure in the manner of Oscar Wilde that is found in some of her early works, in *Audrey Craven* (1897), and in parts of *Superseded* and *The Judgment of Eve*.

In *The Combined Maze,* Rannie Ransome, the son of an inebriate chemist and a draper's daughter, lives a drab life relieved by sessions at the London Polytechnic Gymnasium where he indulges his ambition to cultivate a superb physique. Feeling vague urges for sex, Rannie falls in love with Violet, a girl who has so much experience behind her that she quickly traps him into marriage. As a result, Rannie is caught in the struggle of acquiring a house and furniture — all of which begin to deteriorate before they can be paid for. When Violet, who has other lovers, finally leaves Rannie, he saves his money for two years so he can divorce Violet and marry his childhood friend, Winky, who has loyally loved him. But, when his father dies, he must use the money to pay his father's debts. After saving for two more years, Rannie has enough money for the divorce; but his wife, broken in health and in spirit, returns to him; and Rannie, thinking she has nowhere to turn, takes her back and surrenders all hope of ever marrying Winky.

In this novel, life is portrayed as being determined by sex and environment and as lacking ultimate meaning. The "combined maze," the maze through which Rannie runs at the London Gymnasium, is the central symbol of the work, the symbol of life's determinism. Rannie says about life, "It was a maze, because you ran it winding in and out like, and combined, because men and women ran in it all mixed up together. They made patterns according as they ran, and the patterns were the plan of the maze. You didn't see the plan. You didn't know it. You just followed."[35] Later, he says, "What do we know about anything? What does it all mean? The whole boomin' show? The combined maze? They shove us into it without our leave. They make us do things we don't want to do and never meant to. I didn't want to care for Violet. . . ."[36]

Not only is Rannie caught in the maze; so also are his father, who drinks for an escape, and Violet, who cannot control her strong sensual nature. In a visit to a zoo, Rannie notices a bird dancing; and the keeper explains, "That's what he does when he goes courtin'. . . . It's nature, that's what it is. Nature's wound him up to go and he goes. You see it's the instinct in him and the time of year."[37] The rather sordid details about the drunk father in the chemist's shop, the harshness of Rannie's life, and the view of sex as an instinct that pushes man in directions not of his own choosing are all naturalistic themes.

Though naturalistic in its details of lower middle-class life with decaying homes and dreary shops, the novel is not by any means a drab one. The sprightly style matches the zestful Rannie, who, in spite of his harsh life, enjoys his workouts at the gymnasium, the devoted love of Winky, and his outings at the zoo and at fairs. The portrait of Rannie, affectionately done, is of a likeable fellow, who, despite all his problems, retains a capacity for joy and for ideals. Although the novel is deterministic and fatalistic, enough hints about what is wrong in society suggest avenues of reform. For example, marriage and divorce laws are criticized in a fashion rarely used by any writer of the era. At a fair, Rannie and Winky watch an exhibit of half-naked savages with the title, "trial marriage." The guide explains, "They try it first and if they don't like it they can chuck it." Rannie exclaims, "It's a rippin' good idea, Winky, shows what a thunderin' lot of sense these simple savages have got. . . . Why they must be hundreds of years ahead of civilization to have thought it all out like that!"[38]

Despite the style and the characterization, the novel is obviously an imitative one, in which not all its tones are fused. The relationship between Winky and Rannie belongs entirely to the world of the ideal: she cares for his children when his wife deserts him, and he faithfully works for four years to earn his divorce and marry her. One detects in the relationship between Rannie and Winky the use of one of Sinclair's favorite beliefs derived from idealistic philosophy — the development of self through sacrifice and struggle. Rannie is at first a likeable, foolish fellow who sets his sights no higher than having a well-developed physique; but, because of his struggles he develops compassion and an understated fineness and nobility. Sinclair uses the naturalistic outlook as a means of exposing the conventional ideas about sex and marriage that impede man's happiness and fulfillment. In using the naturalistic style, she tried to be objective; but detachment was difficult for her, and her affection for Rannie and Winky becomes evident.

The reviewer in the *Times Literary Supplement* who found some of the details in the novel offensive, wrote that "Few novelists, now that full liberty of speech is given them, are able to deny themselves the luxury of indulging it to the full, and May Sinclair has in all artistic seriousness, given us, what seems now inevitable, an obstetric case. We could have supplied this and one or two of the incidents of Violet's progress from the imagination." This reviewer also registered mild surprise that a novelist could write with sympathy about the lower middle class: "These are people who the superior person or novelist is inclined to find ridiculous; and they are indeed hard to understand being bound by many of the conventions of the more comfortable classes and by the sordid difficulties of the manual worker."[39]

VIII   *Novels on Marriage and H. G. Wells*

Many of Sinclair's realistic novels can be compared to the novels of H. G. Wells because of their characters and subject matter. Rannie seems to be modeled after the heroes of H. G. Wells's novels of lower middle-class life, such as Lewisham, Kipps, and Mr. Polly. Like them, Rannie is zestful and genial; and, like them, he is trapped in a bad marriage and cramped by poverty and by the restrictive social conventions. Moreover, the subject of all May Sinclair's realistic novels, that of marriage and the relationship between the sexes, is also the subject of at least four of H. G. Wells's novels published in this same period — *The New Machiavelli, Marriage, The Passionate Friends,* and *The Wife of Sir Isaac Harman.* The aim of both writers was to air the subject of marriage and to cut through some of the cant and hypocrisy surrounding it.

In these novels of marriage — ones more justly considered novels about marital incompatibility — both writers depicted some of the difficulties, frustrations, and conflicts that exist in marriage and criticized the social conventions that created and perpetuated these problems. Both writers depicted the state of muddleheadedness and ignorance, sanctioned by society's insistence upon sexual purity, in which most people marry; and, as a result, they try to build for life on the foundations of awakening sexual feelings. Such is the start of Rannie's married life, as is that of Lewisham in *Love and Mr. Lewisham* and George Ponderevo in *Tono-Bungay.* Both writers saw as an evil state of affairs woman's complete dependence on marriage for personal fulfillment and her lack of any outside meaningful work. H. G. Wells showed that the only outlets for creativity and personal satisfaction that were provided for middle-class women, relieved of the care of their children by governesses and servants, were those of dressing up, of keeping well-appointed homes, and giving successful dinner parties. In *Marriage,* Wells showed that these approved interests for women could estrange the couple and create problems; and, in *The Wife of Sir Isaac Harman* and in *The Passionate Friends,* Wells treated this problem more extensively through his two woman protagonists, both of whom are deeply frustrated and unhappy because the socially approved outlets for women of their rank are too flimsy and too superficial to satisfy them. Sinclair touched on the same problem of woman's complete dependence on marriage and lack of any other really meaningful outlets: Mrs. Tyson is utterly devastated by her husband's rejection because of the absence of anything else in her life; and, since the leisured Anne Majendie can only fill her spare time with church work and parsons, she intensifies her morbid ideas of purity and holiness and thereby estranges her husband.

Both Wells and Sinclair saw the ideal relationship between men and women in marriage as a balance between companionship and sex. In Wells's words, a wife should be the "sister-lover" of her husband rather than the submissive, ignorant child-wife who was traditionally favored. Sinclair suggested the same ideal of companionship and love such as exists between Rannie and Winky, and she was opposed to the plaything that Mrs. Tyson is for her husband, to the sex object that Violet is for Rannie, and to the pure spiritual role that Anne Majendie adopts in her marriage. Both writers were concerned with giving sex its proper recognition in marriage; and, as a result, Capes in *Ann Veronica*, Remington in *The New Machiavelli*, and George Ponderevo in *Tono-Bungay* find their wives' restraints and inhibitions irksome, just as Anne Majendie almost destroys her marriage with her ideal of purity.

Vincent Brome has written that "The freedom of the sexes in the twentieth century, the rational attitude towards sexuality, was first made articulate by Wells."[40] Sinclair labored in the same vineyard; and, though these problem novels are now dated, they did help gain acceptance for healthier and more fulfilling ideas about marriage and the relationship between the sexes, and they did help bring sex into literature, if not as an activity, at least as a topic for examination and discussion. Gaining acceptance for discussion of sex in the novel was not a mean achievement when one considers that at least one great writer, Thomas Hardy, was probably silenced as a novelist because of the vituperative reviews his novels received for some frankness about sex.

Sinclair shows tolerance for the woman who breaks the sexual code when she draws Majendie's two mistresses sympathetically and views them as being in certain respects superior to his wife, a pure woman. "One counts by one's power of loving," she wrote in that book.[41] She did not advocate as openly as Wells sexual freedom for the single woman (as Wells seemed to do in *Ann Veronica* and *The New Machiavelli);* but, on the other hand, she was equally bold when she suggested the desirability of trial marriages in *The Combined Maze.* On the whole, however, Sinclair, the older writer, was somewhat more traditional in her outlook; for at times, she did idealize the altruistic, self-sacrificing woman, such as Mrs. Tyson, Winky, and Aggie.

Sinclair and Wells admired and discussed each other's novels, and at times they buoyed each other up against reviewers' criticisms for their lack of reticence.[42] In 1911 Sinclair publicly defended the *English Review* which had been criticized for serializing Wells's "erotic" novel, *The New Machiavelli,* and which was currently under attack by the *Spectator* for an outspoken article by Frank Harris.[43]

If the subject of Sinclair's realistic novels is the same as Wells's prewar problem novels, there are also important differences. From the beginning, Wells's prose was more modern, sparer, and easier than that of Sinclair, who only gradually began to reach such a style in *The Combined Maze.* She seems, however, the more careful craftsman, as befits one who had been influenced by James. Unlike Wells, who in his problem novels tended to cast himself in the chief role, Sinclair remained more impersonal and more aloof from her characters. Although she at times also seems to be lecturing the reader through the dialogue of her characters, she tended to hold this tendency in check; she never, like Wells, devoted whole pages and even chapters to a discussion of social issues. In a letter to Wells, Sinclair found fault with *The New Machiavelli* because "the ideas run away with it."[44] Moreover, she showed in her novels a greater sensitivity to the poetic and symbolic nature of language; and she used this device to make her points instead of direct statement.

Sinclair went on to do her best work in her psychological novels, and it is instructive to ask why Sinclair developed in this direction while Wells did not. Obviously, Sinclair's reading of the new psychology, which she immediately recognized as a means of ameliorating social problems, had much to do with the new direction taken by her novels. In contrast, Wells never came under the influence of the new psychology; indeed, he criticized it in 1913 for being taken over by "pedants"; and he called it "scholastic," "speculative," "ignorant," and "intellectual." He then stated that, "Instead of experience and accurate description and analysis it begins with the rash assumption of elements and starts out upon ridiculous synthesis."[45] Wells had the scientist's mistrust of the "new psychology," but Sinclair's background in philosophy made her more receptive to it. Wells wrote of the "mental hinterland" that the Fabians ignore and that is so basic to human life,[46] but he was too concerned in his own novels with his own beliefs and with his own programs for improving the human lot to bring that hinterland into his art. And, though Sinclair in her psychological novels created for her characters a more self-sustained and fuller existence, she remained, like Wells, a social critic whose desire to change human conduct and social conventions at times obtruded to the detriment of her art.

With the exception of *Superseded*, which is still a moving novel, and *The Combined Maze*, which is as good as one of H. G. Wells's minor novels, most of May Sinclair's realistic novels are dated and perhaps only of interest for the light they shed on the plight of women in the late Victorian world. In these novels, Sinclair was trying to work her way through some of the Victorian cant about women and marriage, a process in which she occasionally fell back on Victorian types, as for example Kitty Tailleur — the prostitute with the pure heart; or Aggie Getty in *The Judgment of Eve* — the self-sacrificing, idealized mother-wife.

Though dated now, the reviews these novels received suggest that Sinclair's rebellion against the matter and manner of Victorian novels was not quixotic. Her egalitarianism, her frankness, and her skepticism — that is, her writing with sympathy and without condescension of lower-class people, her frankness about sex, and her skepticism about society's institutions — were looked upon with surprise, if not shock, in 1913. In these realistic novels, Sinclair made her transition from the Victorian to the modern novel. By 1913, the subplots of *The Divine Fire*, the effusive prose, the acceptance of society's institutions, and the optimism about man's destiny have disappeared from her works. In these realistic novels, the theme of the sexual and emotional fulfillment of men and women and the stress on the impediments to that fulfillment created by conventional views of women, of marriage, and of the family prepare the way for the themes of her psychological novels, *The Three Sisters*, *Mary Olivier* and *Life and Death of Harriett Frean*.

CHAPTER 4

The Three Sisters

I *Psychoanalysts*

MAY Sinclair's novel, *The Three Sisters* (1914), marks a break
from her prewar ones. With this novel, she moved from the
world of external environment to the inner world of feelings and of
the subconscious, from the world of Wells to the world of D. H.
Lawrence. To a certain extent, one can argue that this change was
the result of the extension of the naturalists' dictum to tell the truth
about life as it had been revealed by science. Arthur Waugh in 1919,
referring to the new tendency in fiction, wrote that "It is, in effect, a
New Realism of the emotions as contrasted with the conventional
realism of conditions and environment."[1] To him, this "New
Realism" stressed "the hidden thoughts and secret sins that make up
the life of the character."[2]

The new science of psychoanalysis, or the "new psychology,"
called attention to the emotions and "hidden thoughts." In the im-
mediate prewar years, many psychoanalytic works were beginning to
be translated and to be written. For example, the November, 1912,
issue of the *Proceedings of the Society for Psychical Research*
featured an article on multiple personalities, another on hysteria,
and a third by Freud on the unconscious. In 1909, a selection of
Freud's papers was published in English;[3] and, in 1910, there
appeared the first translation of a complete work by Freud, *Three
Contributions to a Theory of Sex.*[4] Even before the works of Freud
were translated, however, works of other psychologists had
familiarized the English public with the subject matter of psychoanalysis. In 1901, for example, Pierre Janet's *The Mental State of
Hystericals* had appeared in English; Havelock Ellis's *Studies in the
Psychology of Sex* had all been published in six volumes between
1897 and 1910. By their frequent references to Freud and to other

psychologists, Ellis's works doubtless did much to familiarize the English public with the new psychology.

In a letter written in 1932, May Sinclair gave 1913 or 1914 as the year in which she first began to study psychoanalysis.[5] However, some of her short stories suggest that she was familiar with psychoanalytic ideas before 1913. She did not have to wait for the translations to appear, since she knew German so well that she had earned her living for a time by translating it. She became an enthusiastic supporter and defender of psychoanalysis because she was convinced of its social usefulness. In 1913, she contributed five hundred pounds and was a founding member of the Medico-Psychological Clinic of London, a public clinic that treated mental disorders by psychoanalysis, among other means.[6] She also wrote a prospectus for the organization and served on its board of management for a number of years.[7]

Sinclair was sympathetic to psychoanalysis because many of its beliefs were ideas to which she was already committed: the idea of the importance of sex, of the harmful effects of repression, and of the value of self-development or self-realization. She regarded psychoanalysis as an ally in the struggle against Victorian values; for, as she stated in an article on Freud and Jung, "At the present moment there is a reaction against all hushing up and stamping down. The younger generation is in revolt against even such a mild form of repression as Victorian Puritanism. And the new psychology is with it."[8] Psychoanalysis was, therefore, the means of eradicating the puritanism that she had criticized in her prewar novels; and she quoted with evident approval Jung's criticism of the two repressive forces of Victorian society — religion and the family: "Jung's quarrel with Christian religion is that besides being a first class engine of repression it has fostered an infantile dependence on God as the father to which man is already too much prone. Parents and man's childish passion for them are the backward forces that retard his development as an individual . . . the conflict with parents must be fought to the finish and the child must win it or remain forever immature."[9]

Psychoanalysis also provided her with the means of transcending the dichotomy between her idealistic view of man as being capable of achieving his self-realization and fulfillment by his own will and her naturalistic view of man as being determined by his environment and his heredity. She saw in psychoanalysis the means by which man could transcend his biological and environmental determinism:

"Psychoanalysis would seem to be the best if not the only method of conversion — the turning around for the ascent toward the sun."[10] While psychoanalysis recognized the determinism of heredity and environment, analysis and sublimation provided the means for freeing man from this determinism or of at least aiding in transcending it.

Because Sinclair tended to interpret psychoanalysis in the light of her idealistic philosophy, she emphasized those psychoanalytic concepts which agreed with her idealistic point of view and questioned those which did not. To her, psychoanalysis reiterated such concepts of idealism as the importance of self-development, the necessity at the same time for self-sacrifice, and a recognition of a hierarchy of values. She liked the psychoanalytic emphasis upon individual self-realization and wrote of the psychoanalysts' "conception of the Individual as a being of immense importance, seeing that just those forces within and without him which arrest and retard his individuality are backward forces."[11] She viewed sublimation in Jung's terms of "sacrifice and rebirth,"[12] and she quoted Jung's statement that "only through the mystery of self-sacrifice is it possible to be born again."[13] She saw in the theory of sublimation evidence of the acceptance of a hierarchy of values, for, in her words, "sublimation is a turning and passing of desire from a less worthy or less fitting object to fix it on one more worthy and more fitting."[14]

In keeping again with her idealistic point of view, she was critical of the psychoanalysts' lack of concern for absolute truth and for a metaphysically comprehensive view of the world. For example, Jung's theory of God as a "split off sum of libido which has activated the God-imago"[15] repelled her. She felt that in mystical experiences, in art, in beauty, and even in love man came in contact with an absolute reality that could not be explained away as a creation of the libido.[16]

Her reading of the psychoanalysts opened up new areas for her art by bringing into prominence man's unconscious drives, his hidden feelings, and the influence of early family relationships in determining his behavior and character. Although, as her early idealistic novels indicate, Sinclair had been interested in psychological problems of self-identity and self-definition, she tended to sweep these problems under the rug by her persistence in seeing all human activity *sub specie aeternitatis* or, more specifically, as illustrating her idealistic creed. For example, her first novel, *Audrey Craven* (1897), brings to the surface certain psychological problems but sub-

sequently ignores them. Audrey Craven, a young woman who
assumes successively different identities, plays the role of an
aesthete, then of an intellectual, and then of a humanitarian; and she
assumes these roles from and for the benefit of the young man she is
at the moment pursuing. But, after the young man has fallen in love
with her, she loses interest, moves on to another identity and another
lover, and leaves behind her a trail of broken hearts.

Between roles, Audrey has some feelings of guilt, of emptiness and
anxiety; but Sinclair did not develop the psychological implications
of her subject, other than relating in one short paragraph that
Audrey lost both parents at an early age and that her father did not
love her mother. Instead, Sinclair viewed Audrey's problem in
specifically religious and philosophical terms. A minister advises
Audrey that, instead of trying to find herself through art, intellectual
pursuits, and service to humanity, she must lose herself to be happy;
she must stop her self-seeking and submerge her will to that of God.
Sinclair seems to be speaking through the minister; for, as she
showed through Rickman's and Frida's struggles for self-identity,
one could find his salvation and his true identity through self-
sacrifice.

Nor did she deal with psychological questions with any greater
depth in her realistic novels. In fact, Sinclair believed that the
realistic method was not suitable for coming to grips with the springs
of human conduct and character. Mr. Wyndham, one of the
characters in *Audrey Craven*, writes a novel about Audrey using the
method of realism; and May Sinclair indicated the novel's
limitations: "She [Audrey] is made up of bits and pieces of people
stuck together . . . but the thing is, what makes them stick? Mr.
Wyndham doesn't go into that, and that's Audrey."[17] In her own
realistic novels, Sinclair limited herself largely to the effects of social
conditions and conventions; for, as she herself pointed out in *Audrey
Craven*, the canons of realism limit the opportunities for delving into
states of mind and for probing into the psychological motivation or
explanation of characters.[18]

II   *Sinclair's Jamesian Short Stories*

Although May Sinclair gave 1913 or 1914 as the year she first read
the psychoanalysts, she wrote between 1908 and 1913 a number of
short stories that show a growing interest in psychology and an indebtedness to Henry James's fiction. She used in many of these
stories James's central intelligence and his dramatic technique of

mutual irradiation. In an introduction to a collection of her short stories published in 1914, she defended these methods of narration which she referred to as "oblique." This method, she wrote,

is difficult because of its severe and embarrassing limitations. But its defects become its qualities where certain limitations happen to be the essence of the desired effect; where motives are dubious and obscure; where the interest of the entire performance lies in how certain things and certain people appeared to the teller of the tale. The way he makes it out, his surmises, his doubts, his divinations, his interferences which would be criminal in direct narration, are lawful and expedient here; they are all part of the game. Hence the eternal fascination of the method for those who love to deal in half lights and obscurities, in things insubstantial, intricate, and ill-defined.[19]

Between 1908 and 1914, Sinclair's interest was beginning to shift to "things insubstantial, intricate, and ill-defined"; and she found James's later methods more suitable for this subject matter than the realism of social conditions she used in *The Combined Maze*. These Jamesian short stories have a more intricate subject matter and are concerned with vagaries of human feelings and with what is going on in the hinterland of the human psyche. These short stories show Sinclair's growing interest in psychology, anticipate her psychological novels, and mirror some Jamesian subjects and techniques.

"The Gift" (1908) is indicative of Sinclair's new emphasis on her characters' inner life, on complex relationships between people, and on the theme of emotional waste; and these interests were to occupy her in all her psychological novels. Some of the themes of this story are Jamesian; and so also is the technique of the story: it is structured in a series of scenes made up of dialogue and narrative that contain the inner thoughts of the two main characters.

In the first scene, a young writer, Freda, receives a visit from a young man, Wilton; and she happily shows him her latest work while he criticizes and encourages her with her "gift." The tone is one of gentle affection and of a delicate, easy sharing. In the next scene, one of Wilton's friends, Julia, comes to visit Freda; and, amid some inconsequential small talk, she warns Freda that Wilton is afraid of women and bolts as soon as he begins to think they want to marry him. The next section is an extended interior monologue in which Freda tries to piece together Julia's motives for this unexpected revelation and to clarify her own feelings for Wilton. She

wonders if Julia is jealous of Wilton's interest in her and is trying to
make her keep her distance or whether Julia is simply motivated by
kindness.

In the following scene between Julia and Wilton, Julia tells Wilton
that Freda is in love with him and that he must marry her. Wilton
thinks that Julia is being absurd and goes to visit Freda to reassure
himself. This scene between Wilton and Freda bristles with em-
barassment, with tension of things unspoken, and with the effort of
each to read between the lines of the other's statements. Freda is intent on letting Wilton known that she has no personal claim on him
and that their relationship is based on his interest in her "gift." But
she keeps insisting on his collaboration in her work so vehemently
and defensively that he concludes Julia must have been right, and he
bolts.

Six months later, Wilton receives word of Freda's death; and the
woman who first sent him to visit Freda summons him and vaguely
holds him responsible for Freda's death. She explains that, since the
doctors said there was no reason why Freda should have died, "She
would have lived well enough if she had wanted to. . . . If you ask
me what she died of I would say she was either scared to death or
starved."[20] In the final scene, Julia is with Wilton and is trying to
comfort him, but he is now repelled by her and haunted by their
behavior toward Freda.

In addition to the technique of narration, other echoes of Henry
James's work appear in this story. Freda's illness and death are
mysterious, like Milly Theale's in James's *Wings of the Dove* and the
effect Freda's death has on Wilton and Julia is similar to the effect of
Milly's death has on Densher and Kate. The ending of Sinclair's
story also reminds one of the ending of James's story "Two Faces,"
for "The Gift" is also a drama of human loneliness and waste, and
Wilton is like some of Henry James's heroes, who are fearful of
human entanglements and who realize too late that by their own
weaknesses they have become betrayers of love.

In 1911, May Sinclair wrote two short stories that show not only
her familiarity with psychoanalysis but also her indebtedness to
James. "The Intercessor" is a ghost story in which a young man
named Garvin takes a room with an uncommunicative, apparently
troubled family, the Falshaws, and begins to hear cries of a young
child in the house. Before long, the ghost of a little girl is haunting
his room; and he eventually realizes that the ghost is Mrs. Falshaw's
dead daughter who was rejected and mistreated by her mother. Mrs.
Falshaw is now tortured by her guilt and by her fear of the ghost.

Garvin feels pity for both Mrs. Falshaw and the ghost; and, because of his pity and his understanding, he acts as the intercessor between the two. Through him, Mrs. Falshaw loses her fear and guilt and can accept the memory of her dead child; and the child-ghost can now rest in the knowledge of its mother's acceptance.

In contrast to Sinclair's earlier fiction, in which the supernatural is used to convey metaphysical truths, she uses the supernatural in this story to reveal emotions of fear and guilt and the darker side of human nature. Like James, Sinclair uses ghosts as representations of states of mind; and, through them, she explores human relationships. The ghost is a personification of the mother's guilt; and the intercessor, Garvin, is essentially doing the work of the psychoanalyst. The first half of the story is strangely affecting, largely because she so vividly created an atmosphere of unknown terror and oppressiveness that surrounds the house and family. The last part of the story, when the intercessor begins to exercise his influence over the mother and child, is somewhat too neat and diagrammatic and is in this respect different from James's use of the occult. In *Mary Olivier,* Sinclair's chief psychological novel, the relationship between the protagonist and her mother follows the same pattern of longing for acceptance and rejection as in "The Intercessor."

In the same year, 1911, Sinclair wrote another short story, "Between the Lines," in which she used the theories of the psychoanalysts more directly. In this charming, funny story, Colonel FitzJames Throgmorton Lumby, a handsome, comfortable, retired bachelor of fifty-five, loves the company of women if they are impossible to marry — if they are either under twenty-five or over fifty; but he falls into the clutches of Miss Manisty, a virago who is determined to marry him, and whose first step is to convince the colonel that he is not looking very well. The colonel agrees to enter the Hospital of Nervous Diseases for a rest cure; and, since Miss Manisty is the matron at the hospital, she begins working on the colonel by suggestion, bullying, and giving him an inadequate diet until he believes in his own illness and is near a state of collapse. She tells him that by not marrying "he had offended the powers of life and they were calling out in him for propitiation."[21] Still not having wrenched a proposal out of him, she takes matters into her own hands and announces their engagement to the hospital staff. When the doctor congratulates a bewildered colonel on his engagement, he takes flight and is rescued from the hospital steps, still clad in his pajamas, by his friend Simpson.

When Simpson learns about what has happened to the colonel, he

attempts to help extricate his friend from a difficult situation; he
concocts for him a story about a previous attachment to a young
woman with an impossible husband — a woman he has always loved
and whose children he is educating. Knowing that the colonel is very
literal minded and not a good liar, Simpson tries to play on his imagination with the story so that his letter to Miss Manisty will be convincing. To his surprise, the colonel is so very much moved by the
story that his letter to the nurse describes an intense though spiritual
union, a perfect though tragic love; and he concludes his letter with
the lines, "I have lived, I have missed nothing, I have lived intensely
and divinely every moment of my life."[22]
    Though the colonel soon recovers from the ravages of the hospital,
Simpson detects a difference in him. He seems more alive but
somewhat sad — he acts as if the vision of a perfect love has made
him aware that his life has lacked something. Simpson accounts for
the change thus:

I'm inclined to think, myself, that the whole thing was written in him
somewhere and could have been read by those queer people who do read
things, you know — between the lines of consciousness, I mean; that it was a
sort of uprush from the submerged depths of Fitz's personality; . . . he gave
out something that was not his and yet in him — perhaps an ancestral passion, an ancestral memory . . . his maternal grandmother, the beautiful Lady
Adelaide, died of an attachment — a previous and unhappy one . . . his vision stayed with Fitz and made him alive and unhappy. . . . Fitz had
offended, mortally and beyond propitiation the Powers of Life. He had been
made aware of wanting and not having what he wanted.[23]

    Simpson's statement shows that by 1911 Sinclair was aware of
Jung's theories and that she was already critical of the tendency of
some of his followers to reduce everything to the libido. When Miss
Manisty uses the term "the powers of life," she is referring to sex;
but, when Simpson uses the term, he means something more complex and touching on the heart and mind of man. In fact, the colonel
uses the term "not having lived" in the same sense as James's
Strether in *The Ambassadors*. Indeed, this story seems to be
Sinclair's delicate and humorous treatment of the subject of "The
Beast in the Jungle," in which one also finds an unlived life, a theme
that is central in all Sinclair's psychological novels.
    A second apparent Jamesian influence is the use of the central in-
telligence, for, as this passage indicates, the story unfolds from Simpson's point of view; he acts as the *ficelle* who takes some minor part

in the action and who draws out the implications of the subject by seeing its possibilities, its overtones and ironies.

Sinclair's *The Three Sisters* touches on some of the themes and situations that appear in these short stories; for she depicted in this novel, as in "The Gift," some bitter and cruel rivalries between women that occur beneath a surface of polite social intercourse. Again, as in "The Gift," the theme of the fear of sex appears, as does the mysterious illness that cannot be explained as a physical one. The protagonist of the novel, Gwenda, is a young woman like James's Isabel Archer in *Portrait of a Lady* (1881): she is open to life and eager for it; but, by her own choice, by her fastidiousness and ignorance of the world, she ends up tragically alone and renounces her opportunities for happiness in the interest of some higher ideal. In fact, like many of James's characters, the protagonists in all three of Sinclair's psychological novels are women whose lives are wasted, who for one reason or another have missed life.

Of course, important differences between this novel and the work of Henry James are evident. Whereas James made Isabel Archer as free as possible in her choices and gave her the widest possible opportunities, Sinclair made Gwenda's opportunities very narrow and restricted by various circumstances in her life: by an authoritarian father and his repressive religion and by the narrow life of the small lonely village in which Gwenda lives. Sinclair's interest was not only in the drama of individual choice, isolated as much as possible from conditioning factors, but also in the depiction and, at least indirectly, the criticism of all the human institutions and conventions that narrow a person's choice and restrict his opportunities for a full, rich life. In short, this and all her subsequent psychological novels are also novels of social criticism. Sinclair also used some of the ideas of psychoanalysis in her novel: one of the minor characters is an example of sex repression and another of hysteria. Unlike Sinclair, Henry James eschewed any textbook psychology.

III *Influence of Hardy and the Brontës*

May Sinclair, on the other hand, captured in this novel a dimension of passion, of emotional force, that one finds in the fiction of Thomas Hardy, the Brontës, and D. H. Lawrence but that one misses in James's novels. In letters dated 1909 and 1910, Sinclair wrote to Hardy that she was rereading his novels; and she found more to admire each time she read *Tess*, for the psychology of Tess "is always, and profoundly, right."[24] Not surprisingly, *The Three Sisters* shows some of the influence of Hardy's works. The fate of Sinclair's characters is determined by circumstances and sex, and the setting in the stark moors is used to suggest the harshness of their lives. Two of her minor characters, who survive and flourish, are rustics who are attuned to nature and are devoid of inhibitions and the superficial gloss of polite society. Her protagonist Gwenda, who is an aspiring character with aesthetic and moral sensitivity, tries to resist nature and is defeated. As in some of Hardy's novels, an antithesis exists between the harsh and strong natural world and the vulnerable, aspiring human one.

Yet the literary influence that is most apparent in Sinclair's novels is that of the Brontës. In addition to an introduction to a reissue of Mrs. Gaskell's biography of Charlotte Brontë in 1908, Sinclair wrote introductions to six Brontë novels for the Everyman edition between 1908 and 1914; and in 1912 she wrote *The Three Brontës*, a biography of the sisters. In her works about the Brontës, Sinclair emphasized the quality of passion that distinguishes their work, their feminist viewpoint, and the power of their psychological analysis. She considered Charlotte Brontë a "master of the psychology of passion";[25] and she described passion as "that quickening flow, that continuous and sustaining breath that made *Jane Eyre* and *Villette* unique in literature."[26] Other phrases that Sinclair used relative to Brontë's "psychology of passion" are "the truth of men and women,"[27] and "the kingdom of the inner life."[28] She contrasted this quality to realism[29] and called it "poetry."[30] Sinclair's psychological novels have the same Brontë quality of intensely alive inner reality that she characterized as passion.

In writing about the Brontës, she often cited their feminism. She described *The Tenant of Wildfell Hall* as "the first presentment of that Feminist novel we all know,"[31] and she wrote that Charlotte Brontë in *Jane Eyre* and in *Shirley* had intended to destroy the Victorian conventional view of woman.[32] Moreover, she considered the most original element in Charlotte Brontë's novels to be their psychological analysis; as she wrote about *Villette*,

The book is flung, as it were, from Lucy's beating heart; it is one profound protracted cry of longing and frustration. This was a new voice in literature. *Villette* was the unsealing of the sacred secret springs, the revelation of all that proud, decorous mid-Victorian reticence most sedulously sought to hide. There is less overt, audacious passion in *Villette* than in *Jane Eyre*, but there is a surer, a subtler and more intimate psychology.

It is a far cry from *Villette* and from the insight of Charlotte Brontë to that of Mr. Henry James. Her emotion, her overmastering sense of the coloured and the concrete, her very prejudices saved her from the excesses of psychological analysis. But in *Villette* she was the first to give to that method the place it holds in the English novel of today.[33]

Sinclair's psychological novels echo both the subject matter and method of Charlotte Brontë's novels, and especially those of *Villette*.[34] The painstaking analysis and revelation of the inward life of women, especially of those in cramped circumstances who are trying to create a viable life for themselves, became the center of all of Sinclair's psychological novels. In many other ways, the Brontës were very much in Sinclair's mind when she was writing *The Three Sisters*. First, the title of her novel calls to mind the title of the biography, *The Three Brontës;* and, like the Brontës, the three sisters are daughters of a clergyman and the setting is the moors of Yorkshire. Gwenda, her protagonist, resembles Emily Brontë (as she is depicted in Charlotte Brontë's *Shirley* and in Mrs. Gaskell's biography) in her love of the moors and in her courage, independence, and love for her sister. One of the minor characters, Jim, starts out in the novel on the model of Branwell Brontë, a weak-willed, ne'er-do-well drinking man.

In the face of the resemblances to the life of the Brontës and to the subject matter and method of their novels, one must conclude that Sinclair's rereading of their novels in preparation for her biography of them had a liberating effect on Sinclair's own art. It is almost uncanny that Sinclair's description of the difference between Charlotte Brontë's early novel, *The Professor*, and her later one, *Jane Eyre*, can be applied to the difference between Sinclair's early novels and her psychological novels; as Sinclair stated, "To come to *Jane Eyre* after *The Professor* is to pass into another world of feeling and of vision. It is not the difference between reality and unreality. The difference is that *The Professor* is a transcript of reality . . . and *Jane Eyre* is reality itself, pressing on the senses."[35]

Sinclair accounted for this difference, not as Charlotte Brontë's previous biographers had done by the supposed affair Charlotte had had with Constantin Heger on her second sojourn to Brussels, but by the influence upon Charlotte of Emily Brontë's *Wuthering Heights*. Sinclair wrote that "It is not possible that Charlotte should have read *Wuthering Heights* without a shock of enlightenment; that she should not have compared it to her own bloodless work; that she should not have felt the wrong done to her genius by her self-repression. Emily had dared to be herself; she had accomplished a stupendous thing by simply letting herself go. And Charlotte, I think, said to herself, 'That is what I ought to have done. That is what I will do next time.' "[36] In fact, the Brontë novels may have had the same liberating effect on Sinclair that she surmised Emily's novel had had for Charlotte.

IV   *Psychoanalytic Ideas in* The Three Sisters

If the example of Charlotte Brontë gave Sinclair the courage to trust herself and to explore the world of passion — "the inner truth of men and women" — psychoanalysis furnished her with an instrument for probing into the inner life of her characters and with a schema for evaluating it. The influence of psychoanalysis is apparent in her emphasis on subconscious drives, on sex as a pervasive force in human life, and on the evils of repression. The novel is both a dramatization of subconscious drives and a novel of ideas that exposes the tyranny of the family and of religion.

The Three Sisters is the story of Mary, Gwenda, and Alice Cartaret, the daughters of a vicar in a small village in the moors of England. When the book opens, the Cartaret family has recently moved to this village, and the three young women are all beginning to fall in love with Steven, the village doctor and practically the only eligible man in the village. Steven falls in love with Gwenda; but, when she realizes that her younger sister Alice has become dangerously ill from unrequited love for Steven, she leaves the village in the hope that Steven will fall in love with Alice. Alice, however, recovers from her illness and from her infatuation with Steven; and she marries a young farmer. In Gwenda's absence, the oldest sister Mary, a pious but scheming woman, succeeds in convincing Steven to marry her. When Gwenda returns six months later, she realizes the futility of her sacrifice and faces a lifetime of emptiness caring for her now invalid father.

The vicar, father of the girls, shows the greatest contrast between conscious behavior and subconscious drives. A man with a strong sensual nature, he is condemned by the flight of his third wife to a life of celibacy. Under the stress of his frustration, the vicar finds both pleasure and revenge in tyrannizing his family: he forbids Alice her piano; insists on family prayers every night; and, most of all, forbids his daughters to be courted by young men. Forced as he is to repress his own sexual nature, he views all sexuality in his daughters with alarm and horror; but, near the end of the narrative, his elaborate system of repressions begins to collapse. When he discovers that Alice has become pregnant by a young farmer and when Gwenda defends her sister, he flies into a rage and suffers a stroke. After his illness, all memory of the incident that brought about the stroke has been effaced from his memory; and he has also changed to a sometimes irritable but mostly kind old man.

The same contrast between conscious acts and subconscious motives is also depicted in the three sisters. Alice is most like her father in that she too has a deep sensual nature; but, unlike him, she is not secretive, for she expresses her emotions as best she can; but she too has little understanding of herself. Irritable and resentful at her father's cloistering her in Garth, she vents on her piano all her pent-up emotions and becomes hysterical when they overwhelm her. She gets back at her father by refusing to eat, until she makes herself sick. When she meets Jim, a simple and earthy farmer, she responds to his warmth and tenderness but fears him and the qualities he possesses and evokes in her.

Mary, the oldest sister, is also a woman driven by her repressed desires. Of the three women, she is the most obedient to her father; and she is also conventional and pious. But, driven by her desire for a husband, she ignores Gwenda's and Steven's love for each other; and, by concealments and innuendoes that she does not seem to admit to herself, she convinces Steven that Gwenda never loved him and traps him into marriage. After her marriage, she betrays herself by always finding it necessary to defend herself to Gwenda — not about the way she betrayed Gwenda's confidence, which she refuses to admit to herself, but about trivial matters.[37]

Unlike the two sisters, Mary and Alice, who act on their drives without a clear knowledge of what they are doing, Gwenda is the least driven. The most intelligent of the three sisters and the most perceptive, she is aware of her feelings and can also act with intelligence and moral will. When Gwenda is told that Alice must either marry or go mad, she feels strong enough to sacrifice Steven; but Gwenda does not completely understand herself. She makes her choice without hesitation "with a strange courage and a sort of spiritual exaltation. . . . Then her heart dragged and tore at her as if it fought against her will to die. But it never occurred to her that this dying of hers was willed by her. It seemed foredoomed, inevitable."[38]

Although Sinclair never states baldly Gwenda's real problem, she has brought upon herself tragic fate by acting too much on the basis of her ideals and too little on the basis of her feelings. Years later, when Steven realizes Mary's perfidy, he wants to make love to Gwenda; but she refuses him. Thinking later about her rejection of him, she wonders why she had refused him: "For Mary? It wasn't for Mary. It was for yourself. For your own wretched soul."[39] She recognizes, therefore, that ideals about her own behavior have stood in the way of satisfying her feelings; and, by the end of the novel, Gwenda realizes the tragic folly of her having sacrificed Steven for Alice and for Mary. She finds escape and solace in her reading — "for there is nothing like thought to keep you from thinking"[40] — and in her mystic communion with nature. But these outlets are not presented as "abundant recompense"; they are forms of sublimation that do not mitigate the tragedy of having lost her lover and of being condemned to the empty life of an aging daughter in her father's house.

This discussion of the subconscious drives and ill-understood motives may make the novel seem a bit like a case history, which it is not. Since the play of subconscious drives is presented rather than stated, the tone of the case history is avoided. Indeed, the closest May Sinclair came to a case history is in her depiction of Alice as a hysteric. When Steven is treating her for her illness, he is at one point reading Janet's *État Mental des Hysteriques;* but, since he did not completely agree with its views, "he picked it up and flung it out of sight as if it had offended him."[41] Steven's diagnosis and prognosis of Alice's illness is more in keeping with Freud's views than with Janet's. Janet, who considered hysteria as predominantly the result of pathological heredity, de-emphasized sex as a cause,[42] but Sinclair seems to follow Freud in depicting it as a defense caused by sexual repression. In contrast to Janet, who believed that hysterics are somehow weak people, calling them at times degenerates,[43] Sinclair followed Freud, who wrote that cases of hysteria can be found in people who are capable and intelligent; she depicted Alice before and after her illness as an essentially intelligent and wholesome young woman driven to hysteria by the repression forced on her by her father.

Sinclair may have drawn on Havelock Ellis's discussion of hysteria in his *Studies in the Psychology of Sex* for some of the details and even for the phraseology. Ellis wrote that hysteria is often found with anemic conditions,[44] that it can be cured by marriage,[45] that it tends to appear among young adults,[46] and that it is caused by "sexual starvation."[47] Alice is described as pale and anemic; Steven says of her, "she's been starved;"[48] and, when she marries, she is completely cured, as Steven predicts.

On the whole, Sinclair's use of psychoanalytic ideas does not follow any literal textbook pattern. She concentrated on the pervasiveness of sexual feelings and emphasized the harmful effects of repression. The strength of the novel lies not in the illustrative use of psychoanalytic ideas but in the vividness and fidelity with which the inner life of women is depicted as they attempt to fulfill themselves in their cramped circumstances.

V *Feminism*

Viewed from this light, the novel is essentially feminist and is a rebuttal to some ideas about women rather commonly held by anti-suffragettes of the time. For example, on the eve of the vote on the Conciliation Bill of 1912 (one extending the vote to some women), the London *Times* devoted three of its columns to a letter to the editor by a doctor, Sir Almroth Wright, in which he argued that women should not be given the vote because of their mental, physical, and moral inferiority. To this doctor, "One would not be very far from the truth if he alleged that there are no good women, but only women who have lived under the influence of a good man."[49] He argued that fifty percent of all women went insane by middle life; that women in favor of the vote were neurotic or bitter old maids; that woman was mentally inferior because of the "reverberations of her physiological emergencies"; and that the only worthy life for woman was as "some good man's wife."[50] The *Times* printed a reply to this letter by May Sinclair in which she avoided the question of woman's nature or abilities and concentrated on the practical argument that some women had to work and that they needed the vote to end their economic exploitation.

One cannot help feeling that she reserved for her novel *The Three Sisters* her more thorough answer to Sir Almroth's views; for she showed through Alice that some women become hysterical neurotics not because of any innate incapacity but because of the strain of repressing their sexual feelings, a repression that society forces on them. Through Mary, she demonstrated that the conventional view of wifehood as the only respectable role for woman robs her of her integrity by driving her to demeaning deceptions and schemes to win a husband. Mary, who fulfills Sir Almroth's ideal of being the wife of a good man, is shown to be given to petty malice and minor

corruptions. Gwenda, who is the most independent of men, is also
the most moral and capable; but the implication of her end is that
women of this type become victims in the world as it is. Alice, the
least moral in Sir Almroth's technical sense, is the one sister who
finally has the most fulfilled life of all.

In the opening scene of the novel, in which the three sisters are sitting in the dining room waiting for evening prayers to begin, Sinclair
communicated the atmosphere of boredom and frustration that op-
presses young women of the middle classes with time heavy on their
hands and with no work or training to fill it. The vicar frowns on
even their most innocent outlets, such as playing the piano or taking
long walks, for he sees his daughters as existing to serve his convenience and comfort. Even Steven, a humane and relatively
enlightened young man, resents Gwenda's having any kind of life
apart from his own: he resents her love for the moors and her failure
in adjusting herself completely to all of his moods. Almost unconsciously, both before and after his marriage, he uses her to boost
his ego. Everyone in the family, including Gwenda herself, takes it
for granted that, as her father's only unmarried daughter, she must
sacrifice any desire for a life of her own and devote herself to being
his housekeeper.

The problems of the dependent woman in late Victorian society
that Sinclair introduced in this novel were real ones, for ample
evidence exists in the memoirs and social histories of the late Victorian and early Edwardian periods about the exploitation of dependent women and about the demeaning lives they frequently led.
Cecil Woodham-Smith in her biography of Florence Nightingale
related the story of Florence Nightingale's favorite cousin, Hilary
Bonham Carter, a sweet-natured young woman and a gifted painter,
who was called home after a year's work in Paris because she "could
not be spared" and "was needed at home,"[51] even though her family
had ample means and numerous servants. When she died years later,
the specter of her wasted life haunted Florence Nightingale, for her
cousin's fate was one she herself had barely escaped. She wrote to a
friend in rage, "There is not a single person, except yourself, who
does not think that Hilary's family were quite right in this most
monstrous of slow murders — and all for what? . . . the Fetishism to
which Hilary has been sacrificed is very dirty and disgusting."[52]

Sinclair did not editorialize about the wastefulness and stupidity
of Gwenda's sacrifice, but she communicated Gwenda's anguish and
the tragedy of having her, the most resourceful and most gifted of

the three sisters, live her life as her father's housekeeper. This exploitation of young women to the fetish of the family was also described by Lawrence Jones in relating the plight of his own sisters. Whereas he was sent to Oxford, his sisters remained at home and were prepared for no work. Nor did the family make any effort to find them husbands. After their mother's death his sisters, "having submitted with adoration to her unconscious demands for unconditional surrender, were now waifs indeed."[53]

As these memoirs indicate, the vicar's demand of unconditional surrender from his daughters was not exceptional at the time. Nor was the hostility of a wife toward her unmarried sister, such as Mary feels toward Gwenda, uncommon. A social historian of the period, W. L. Burns, referred to "the designs so often attributed to the wife's sister."[54] Since the status and self-esteem of a woman were dependent entirely on her being a wife and mother, it is no wonder that bitter rivalries developed between women. To the married woman, single women, especially those in close proximity to her husband, were still threatening. The Deceased Wife's Sister Act (not repealed until 1907) forbidding a woman from marrying her deceased sister's husband suggests that wives were jealously guarding their position against the threat of single women, often dependent sisters living with them.

VI *D. H. Lawrence*

Sinclair's criticism of restrictive family life, her depiction of the tragic position of women, and her use of psychoanalytic ideas place *The Three Sisters* in the tradition of the novel of ideas. As such, the novel offers a rich social history of late Victorian and Edwardian society and values; but this narrative is also a subjective one that vividly captures emotional detail and the inner essence of people by going beyond the surface of social man to his more submerged and inarticulate self. In this respect, the novel is not a realistic novel; by borrowing some of the terminology that Sinclair used to describe the novels of the Brontës, one can characterize *The Three Sisters* as a novel of "poetry," of "passion," of the "inner truth of men and women."

As such, the novel has symbolist and mythical qualities. The three sisters and the relationships they form with their lovers are expressions of three different kinds of love. A critic at the time of its publication, responding to the mythical quality of the work, associated the love of Demeter with Mary; of Artemis with Gwenda;

and of Aphrodite with Alice.[55] In dealing with different kinds of love, Sinclair's novel seems to have anticipated many of D. H. Lawrence's themes. Indeed, enough similarities exist between this novel and Lawrence's works to suggest that he may have been influenced by it. *The Three Sisters* is, therefore, a transitional novel in the history of English literature because its source is Charlotte Brontë and its influence leads to D. H. Lawrence.

Both *Women in Love* and *The Three Sisters* deal with different kinds of love: in *Women in Love*, the rightness of the love of Ursula and Birkin is contrasted to the wrongness of the love of Gudrun and Gerald; and, in *The Three Sisters*, the love of Alice and Jim is contrasted in the same way to the love of Mary and Steven. Mary's and Steven's love has a deadening quality, for Steven is obsessed after his marriage with social climbing, with acquiring property, and with smothering domesticity. He had become a comfortable person; but all that was fine, alive, and vibrant in him has been lost. Jim and Alice, who trust most to their instincts and who go least by conventions, are both happy and fulfilled.

Sinclair's depiction of the courtship of Gwenda and Steven has many similarities with Lawrence's of Ursula and Birkin: both are vital relationships, but both are never free from tension. At times, Gwenda and Steven quarrel fiercely with each other; but they never do so about anything that is either stated or clearly understood by them. Gwenda has a core of individuality that she cannot submerge in her relationship with Steven, and her self-contained and aloof quality exasperates Steven. In *Women in Love*, the tension between Ursula and Birkin has a similar source; but, in this relationship, the woman, not the man, wants complete possession.

As in Lawrence's *The Rainbow* and *Women in Love*, the moon is used in *Three Sisters* as a symbol of the antagonism between men and women. From the beginning and consistently throughout the novel, Gwenda is identified with the moon: "She flashed by like a huntress, like Artemis carrying the young moon in her forehead."[56] After Gwenda and Steven have met, they take long walks on the moors together; and, when the moon is out, Steven feels Gwenda's remoteness: "From the turn of her head and the even falling of her feet he felt her unconsciousness of his existence. And her unconsciousness was hateful to him. It wiped him clear out of the universe of noticeable things."[57] When the moon is not in the sky, Steven feels that the time is so much more auspicious for him that he proposes to Gwenda. Lawrence in *The Rainbow* and in *Women in*

Love used moon imagery in a similar way; for, when Ursula and Skrebensky make love in the moonlight, Skrebensky feels resentful toward Ursula and overpowered by her. In the "moony" episode in *Women in Love*, when Birkin feels antagonistic toward Ursula, he throws stones at the image of the moon in the pool.[58]

Another theme that appears in *The Three Sisters* that Lawrence also used in works subsequently published is based on the contrast between the asexual, conventional, and sterile life and the fruitful, tender, sexual life. In *The Three Sisters*, the vicar stands for the former and Jim, the farmer, for the latter. The opening scene in the vicar's house is suffused with an atmosphere of gloom, resentment, and supression as the three sisters wait for the hated evening prayers to begin. This scene is followed by one of Jim in the barn nursing his sick mare back to life — a scene of warmth and tender passionate concern. Jim acts throughout the novel as the foil to the vicar who stands for repressed passion that emerges in devious and sinister ways. Jim is the natural man who drinks, likes women, and has none of the encrusted and deadly hypocrisies of the vicar. The two men lock in a deadly combat over Alice; and she stands between the two because she loathes her father's house but is fearful of Jim's sexuality. Jim makes love for the first time with Alice in his barn; and, when Jim claims Alice at her father's house, the vicar suffers his stroke and is defeated. Years later, Alice is a serene and fulfilled woman in Jim's house.

Lawrence also used this contrast as his main theme in many of his works and, like Sinclair, expressed the contrast both through people and places. For example, in his short story, "The Blind Man," Lawrence contrasted the sexual, vital blind man in his barn with the cerebral sterile friend. In the house, the blind man is ill at ease; but the friend is effective; in the barn, the friend cringes; but the blind man conquers. In *Lady Chatterly's Lover*, the same contrast is expressed: Lord Clifford, the house, and the sterile life are set in opposition to Mellors, the animals, the barn, and the vital life; and Connie, like Alice, flees from the sterility of the house to the life-giving farmer.

Because of these many parallels between *The Three Sisters* and Lawrence's works, it seems likely that Sinclair's novel influenced Lawrence. The chronology of the works involved does not preclude an influence since all of Lawrence's works mentioned were written after Sinclair's novel; but the strongest evidence that Lawrence was influenced by Sinclair's novel is provided, perhaps, by a comparison between a 1911 version of Lawrence's story, "Two Marriages," and the rewritten version of it that was published as "Daughters of the Vicar"[59] two months after Sinclair's *The Three Sisters*. In both versions of the story, Lawrence contrasted the attitudes to love of two sisters. The younger, Louisa, more impulsive and practical, falls in love with a young collier, Alfred Durant; but the older sister, Mary, more intellectual and idealistic, marries an accomplished intellectual man who is emotionally dead. The germ of Lawrence's story is very similar to Sinclair's 1907 novella, *The Judgment of Eve*, in which the more idealistic sister marries the more intellectual man and is unhappy, while her more practical younger sister makes a happy marriage with a young farmer.

In "Daughters of the Vicar," Lawrence made a number of additions to "Two Marriages" which echo Sinclair's *The Three Sisters* and which strongly suggest that Lawrence was influenced by Sinclair's novel. In the second version, Lawrence added certain details to Alfred's character that Sinclair had used in connection with Jim in *The Three Sisters*. In the second version, Alfred, like Jim, has a musical voice and sings in the choir of the village church; before Louisa falls in love with Alfred when she is told that he has gone away, her first thought is that she is going to miss hearing his voice in the choir. In *The Three Sisters*, the first thing about Jim that impresses Alice is his musical voice; and, at her request, he joins the choir. In the second version, Alfred puts Louisa on a plane higher than himself: he considers her "all that was beyond him, of revelation and exquisiteness. All that was ideal and beyond him."[60] Jim has the same feelings about Alice: she becomes associated in Jim's mind with the singing in the choir of the church, and she becomes a part of the "impalpable web of his dreams, the divine and delicate things his grosser self let slip."[61]

In the second version, after Alfred's mother dies, he begins to deteriorate — neglecting to wash himself and taking up his former drinking habits (in the earlier version he is a teetotaler) — until Louisa declares her love for him and he regains his pride in himself. Jim also stops drinking after he falls in love with Alice. In the second version, Lawrence added a scene in which Alfred has dinner with Louisa and her family and is very uncomfortable: "But he did not want to eat — that troubled him, to have to eat in their presence."[62] In *The Three Sisters*, when Alice calls on Jim, he makes tea for her but refuses to sit down and eat with her. In the later version, Lawrence added the scene in which Alfred asks Louisa's father for permission to marry her and in which her sister, Mary, defends the couple against the criticisms of her father. This scene echos a similar scene in *The Three Sisters* in which Gwenda defends Alice and Jim against her father.

Lawrence may also have come to see some of the psychoanalytic implications of his story more clearly through Sinclair's novel. In the earlier version, Lawrence had written about Mrs. Lindley, the mother of the girls, who suffers because of the family's poverty and the refusal of the colliers to accept her: "Gradually she retired into an invalid's sofa, her only refuge from overwhelming mortification of poverty, worry and insult."[63] In the later version, with perhaps the example of Sinclair's vicar in mind, he wrote about Mrs. Lindley: "Gradually broken by the suppression of her violent anger and misery and disgust, she became an invalid and took to her couch."[64] In the early version he depicted the relationship between the Lindley parents and their children as cold and restrained without mentioning any repression. In the later version he echoed the vicar's attitude to his children when he added that the Lindleys were "bitterly repressing and pruning their children into gentility."[65]

Sinclair's novel also helped Lawrence sharpen the focus of his story. "Two Marriages" ends with Alfred's mother asking Louisa to marry her son and with Louisa's thinking that perhaps he will not ask her. In fact, the title "Two Marriages" seems to refer to the contrast between the marriages or the families of the Lindleys and the Durants: the one is middle class, cold, and religious; the other, working class, emotional, intense, and warm. In "Daughters of the Vicar," Lawrence, by developing the courtship of Louisa and Alfred until their marriage, focused more sharply on the contrasting love relationships of the two sisters.

Lawrence, however, nowhere acknowledged Sinclair's influence. In a letter dated 1925, his references to Sinclair were surly and hostile; for the gist of his comments was that he did not think highly of her work, and he also included derogatory comments about her appearance and person.[66] Sinclair, who had always written favorably on Lawrence's works,[67] had referred to the "profound vitality" of his poetry; and, in 1915, she and Arnold Bennett were the two English writers who protested the suppression of Lawrence's *The Rainbow*. Sinclair was probably countering the charges of obscenity and indecency that had been made against the novel when she later wrote that "The suppression of this book was a crime, the murder of a beautiful thing."[68]

Lawrence, however, was not known for his gratitude either to his benefactors or to the writers from whom he drew inspiration for his own works. For example, in his essay about Hardy, he also sought to minimize an influence that had been strong. Lawrence doubtless knew *The Three Sisters* and most probably had read it; for he wrote in a letter of 1916 that "I thought of calling this novel of mine, *Women in Love*. But I don't feel sure of it. It was *The Sisters* but May Sinclair having had *Three Sisters*, it won't do."[69]

In part, some of the similarities between *The Three Sisters* and some of Lawrence's subsequent works can be accounted for by the fact that both writers were influenced by the same novelists and also by the same advanced thinkers of their time. In addition to Thomas Hardy, as Emile Delavenay has pointed out, Lawrence was also influenced by the works of Charlotte Brontë, who had been one of his favorite authors since his adolescence.[70] Like Sinclair, Lawrence, in his criticism of the repressive and materialistic values of the middle class and in his desire to liberate the individual from puritan inhibitions, drew from the works of Havelock Ellis, both directly and indirectly through the works of Edward Carpenter.[71] Some of the similarities between Sinclair's novel and the works of D. H. Lawrence may also have been due to similarities in the sensibilities of the two writers; for, as Curtis Brown, the literary agent for both writers, commented in his memoirs, "D. H. Lawrence and May Sinclair had the burning glass kind of mind. Whatever caught their eye would cause a concentration of rays. It might be the wrong thing, but it began to crisp and burn as soon as those intense rays were focused on it, whether it was a sex episode, or a quarrel with a publisher or an agent."[72]

VII *Evaluation*

Whatever the influence on D. H. Lawrence may have been, *The Three Sisters* is a powerful and intensely realized novel. The novel is structured around scenes of intensely realized moments — the sisters' waiting for prayers to begin; Essy, the servant, spilling the milk in the vicar's room; Jim's nursing the mare; Essy's telling her mother of her pregnancy. The method is scenic and dramatic, and the themes are realized through images and symbols rather than through exposition. The vicarage and Jim's farm are the symbols of the two polarities of repression and death versus emotion, sex, and life through which the theme of the novel is expressed. The vicarage, like all the houses in the village Garth, is made of stone roofs and walls "blackened by the wind and rain as if fire had passed over them."[73] By the end of the story, Gwenda is trapped in Garth and in the vicarage; and the bleakness, darkness, and hardness of these stone houses become expressions of her own desolate life. In contrast to Gwenda, all the vital characters in the novel — Alice, Jim, Essy, and Essy's mother — are associated in one way or another with Jim's farm. Essy spills the milk in the vicar's study, for nourishing life-giving emotions cannot survive in his house. The vicar humiliates the pregnant Essy and dismisses her, just as he later tries to humiliate the pregnant Alice.

In addition to the vicarage and Jim's farm, the third most frequently recurring symbol is that of the moon, with which Gwenda is associated. The moon is a symbol of her Artemis virginal qualities; of her fastidiousness in refusing Steven for the sake of Alice and then Mary; of her intellectual qualities and her independence that Steven finds exasperating. But the moon is also associated with death, for it shines on the night when Jim's father is dying. Gwenda's independence, fastidiousness, and moral superiority are also related to death; for these qualities cut her off from her feelings for Steven. When she makes her choice to leave Steven for Alice's sake, Sinclair referred to Gwenda's death wish: "Then her heart dragged and tore at her as if it fought against her will to die. But it never occurred to her that this dying of hers was willed by her. It seemed foredoomed. . . ."[74] Her decision brings both her and Steven a kind of death; for, although Steven is comfortable, he forgets not only his love for Gwenda but also his dreams of specializing in medicine and of establishing a more demanding and rewarding practice in Liverpool: he becomes, therefore, only the husk of the man he once was. In contrast, Gwenda remembers their love and the vital young Steven and she suffers; but the ordeal of her suffering seems to confer on her a more profound consciousness. On a visit to Jim's farm, she sees some flowering thorn trees and is ecstatically moved by the sight, by their "unearthly beauty."[75] It is as if her suffering (thorn trees) is capable of bearing its own kind of blossom in greater understanding. She realizes now the truth in Steven's jibe when he was courting her, "You are too clever, too clever."[76] Her pride in her own moral and intellectual superiority that made her renounce Steven for the sake of her sisters is now a bitter memory.

The Three Sisters has a pulsating energy and immediacy that are new in Sinclair's work, and one almost feels a release of powers long held back. One can partly account for this change by the effect of the

Brontë novels on her and by her reading of the psychoanalysts. Her acquaintance with psychoanalysis possibly was more than theoretical since Dr. Hector Munro, the medical director of the Medico-Psychological Clinic, was also Sinclair's physician.[77] In her will, she left him her Jung books; and, in 1914, she dedicated a book of short stories to the staff of the Medico-Psychological Clinic. Whether or not with her physician's help, Sinclair used psychoanalytic concepts to come to terms with her own life in her autobiographical novel, *Mary Olivier*. Gwenda's predicament was not unlike Sinclair's, for Sinclair spent her life until she was almost forty looking after her invalid mother. She was a very pretty young woman, with pleasing features, a full face, abundant dark hair, and lively expressive eyes. Since Sinclair probably rejected more than one Steven for her mother's sake, she was perhaps understanding and setting in perspective in *The Three Sisters* certain aspects of her own experience.

In 1909, while writing *The Creators*, she had also suffered a serious illness, one which may have led her to look into herself and try to come to terms with her past. In one letter to the editor, she promised to meet the next deadline; but, "It all depends on whether I go mad or not."[78] Shortly after this letter, she became ill, was in a nursing home for three weeks, and wrote two letters that emphatically asserted that her editor was not to believe "the rumors that I had a nervous breakdown."[79] As one of her contemporaries described Sinclair's illness, she was "found alone in a high fever, stretched on a divan, absolutely helpless, and having tasted nothing for several days."[80] In a letter to Thomas Hardy in 1909, Sinclair explained that she would not be able to go cycling with him because she had been sick and had strained her heart.[81] She had apparently worked herself to exhaustion, while following, perhaps, Gwenda's philosophy that thought keeps one from thinking. Not until after Sinclair began her association with the Medico-Psychological Clinic in 1913 did she start to write about experiences closer to her own. (In regard to this change in her, it is interesting to note that she used psychoanalytic terminology to account for the difference in Charlotte Brontë after her *The Professor;* for Sinclair explained that Charlotte "felt the wrong done to her genius by her self-repression."[82])

In certain respects, *The Three Sisters* is a dated book. By today's tastes, Sinclair at times overwrote and was effusive, especially when she was trying to communicate some of the stark and awesome qualities of the Garth countryside. The reader is drawn into Gwenda's plight, the poignancy of a woman of superior gifts having such little scope given to her; but, in certain respects, Gwenda is too self-consciously drawn to contrast with the Victorian stereotype of woman. Physically robust, she walks fifteen miles a day for fun; and, morally enlightened and discriminating, she lectures her father on his dismissal of the pregnant servant Essy — "Better to do what Essy's done than do mean or cruel things"[83] — and also defends the weak and bullied Alice against her father. Though Gwenda's own views are so enlightened and so forgiving about transgressions against conventional morality, she is herself the soul of rectitude, honor, and self-denial. At times, like Sinclair herself, Gwenda seems as much a product of Victorian values as a rebel against them.

What was new about the novel in its time that is still compelling today is its emphasis on feminine sexual emotion and on man-woman relationships. However, this novel appeared in the first few months of the war; and, as a result, it did not receive the attention it deserved. The review in the *Athenaeum,* for example, dealt more with the fact that Sinclair was with an ambulance unit in Belgium than it did with the novel itself. Ezra Pound, who wrote that this novel was "the best she has done," then related that Sinclair was "pulling wounded off the field" on the Belgian front. He also noted her usual adroitness in avoiding the limelight: "She has kept her name out of the papers, although everybody else has been appearing in large photos."[84]

CHAPTER 5

War Interval

T HE effect of the war on May Sinclair's novels was indeed
unfortunate in more direct ways, for the novels she wrote during
the war years, *Tasker Jevons* and *A Tree of Heaven*, represent a
backtracking in her development as a novelist: they lack the
emotional detail and the rendering of the life below the level of
everyday social experience that distinguish *The Three Sisters*. As
Wyndham Lewis observed, "the realities that had begun to peep out
in 1914 in England were submerged"[1] during the war years; and, in
May Sinclair's case, her eagerness to contribute to her country's war
efforts through her novels betrayed her to some facile, superficial,
and sentimental writing.

I   A Journal of Impressions in Belgium

Sinclair spent seventeen days in September and October, 1914, at
the Belgian front with the Motor Field Ambulance Corps. The corps,
organized and led by Dr. Hector Munro, consisted of thirteen
English volunteers and was accepted for service at the front by the
Belgian Red Cross. According to Mrs. Belloc-Loundes, not always
completely reliable as a source, Sinclair had donated her life's saving
to help finance the corps.[2] Sinclair acted as the secretary of the
group, as the treasurer, and as the official journalist who wrote articles for the *Daily Chronicle* to help with the expenses of the corps.

Initially, Sinclair refused Dr. Munro's invitation to join his ambulance unit on the grounds that she was not a journalist and not a
nurse; therefore, she would not "go and look on and make copy out
of the sufferings I cannot help."[3] After Dr. Munro accused her of being afraid, she accepted his challenge, only to find that she felt real
terror at the thought of the possible sights and sounds of war. But,
after she reached the front lines, she discovered to her relief that,
while picking up the wounded and facing other dangers, she ex-

perienced a sense of intense happiness and had what can perhaps be described as a religious experience — a sense "of touching Reality at its highest point in a secure and effortless consummation."[4]

Very quickly Dr. Munro and Sinclair clashed, for he apparently found her to be irritating and insubordinate. For all her outward diffidence, Sinclair was a woman with an iron will and a mind of her own who found it impossible to obey orders blindly. On one occasion, when Dr. Munro refused to take two wounded Germans on the ambulance, she and two other women in the corps, feeling that "wounded are wounded," simply ignored him and loaded them. The relationship between herself and Dr. Munro was also strained by the fact that he kept taking to the front with him an eighteen-year-old girl whose mother had allowed her to join the corps only on the condition that she would not be taken to the front lines. After seventeen days Sinclair was sent home by Dr. Munro, ostensibly to raise funds. But when she tried to return to Belgium she discovered that he had placed an embargo on her passport through the War Office and had thereby forbidden her return to Belgium.[5]

This insidious deception obviously rankled when she wrote the journal; but, since she did not mention it, she was probably seeking to minimize the element of personal grievance in an account of much greater human suffering. Yet, because she tried to record her impressions as honestly as she could, her own feelings of anger and resentment often appear. Hence the reader, who does not know the incident that provoked her feelings, is bound to be somewhat puzzled by what seems to be an unjustified petulance and grievance. In spite of the humiliation and pain that this incident must have caused her, Sinclair remained loyal to the corps by dedicating the journal to the corps and by mentioning more than once Dr. Munro's heroism at the front.

The experience also left her with a sense of her inadequacy to take part in a life of action. In reference to the episode in which she disobeyed Dr. Munro by loading the wounded Germans, she wrote that it was "rank insubordination," that the Commandment had been entirely right, but that "it was one of the wrong things I would do again to-morrow."[6] In the poem of dedication to the corps, she began, "I do not call you comrades,/You,/who did what I only dreamed." She ended the stanza, "For I have done no more than Dream."[7] Perhaps this sense of having failed through direct action to make a contribution to the war made her use her pen for this purpose in her two subsequent novels.

Sinclair's powers of observation as a novelist are evident in many of her descriptions, such as those of the gunfire she hears for the first time at the front and of the two days she spends helping to feed in shifts that go on all day the 10,500 refugees their ration of two slices of dry bread and bowl of coffee. She is disarmingly frank about many of her impressions and reactions. As she watches the refugees with their wounded among them sleeping on the floor, they seem apathetic, stunned, and inhuman. As for her own and others' reaction, their "c'est triste," at first genuinely felt, soon becomes merely a habitual empty response. She spends one night nursing a dying English boy who is pathetically happy at having someone with him who speaks his language. She records her frustration at not having had any medical training to help her look after him better and her relief when morning came and the Belgian nurse relieved her of this "intolerable responsibility."[8]

She captures the aimlessness and confusion when the corps joins the retreat; for rumors are rife; and, as orders are followed by counterorders, a great hubbub of purposeless rushing about occurs. In the retreat, the Ambulance Corps, a few miles ahead of the advancing German troops, evacuates the wounded from a convent while the nuns quietly go about their habitual tasks. Sinclair records her sadness at leaving the convent: "Here you saw a carefully guarded and fragile loveliness on the eve of its dissolution. . . . And you felt that they [the nuns] and their faces and their gestures were impermanent, that this highly specialized form of holiness had continued with difficulty until now, that it hung by a single thread to a world that had departed very far from it. . . . We shall never know all that the War has annihilated."[9]

Sinclair returned from Belgium so deeply moved by the sufferings of the Belgians and so thoroughly committed to the war effort that she worked for the Commission for Relief in Belgium and contributed to it the royalties from *A Journal*. For all her commitment to the war, she did not join in the more extreme forms of the war enthusiasm; indeed, she wrote in 1918 to Bertrand Russell expressing her sorrow about his having been sent to prison for his pacifism.[10] In the early months of the war, a fervid if not hysterical series of letters to the *Times*, to which some distinguished writers such as H. G. Wells and Conan Doyle contributed, exhorted the civilian population to take up arms, even if only shotguns and carving knives, to defend their homes against Germans. Sinclair, in a letter to the *Manchester Guardian*, protested that these views were dangerous;

for, if civilians shot soldiers, against the Hague conventions of war, they would only bring about the same severe reprisals by the Germans that had occurred in Belgium.[11]

After the war, Sinclair tried to make known not only the appalling conditions in Europe but also her country's responsibility to help alleviate them. Since she did not share most of her countrymen's spirit of vengeance against Germany, she wrote an article in 1920 that appealed for contributions to the Save the Children Fund, which had grown out of the Fight the Famine Council, a Quaker organization that exerted pressure on the allies to lift their blockade against Germany during the war and to do so for the humanitarian reason that the blockade was causing a terrible famine among the civilian population. In her article, Sinclair described the terrible poverty in Germany, Poland, and other countries in Europe; and she warned that, unless the English did something to alleviate these conditions, "we should bring on our heads . . . the commercial and industrial collapse of half Europe." She pointed out that, although the blockade was a military necessity at the time of the war, the English were still responsible for its results. To allow such conditions to prevail, she argued would create "the danger of a war more terrible than any we have yet seen."[12]

Not surprisingly, the war dominated the novels she wrote during those years. As her journal shows, her most persistant memory of the front had been of the great courage and the presence of mind that so many otherwise ordinary people revealed under fire. In her war novels, she drew on this memory and on her own feelings of a kind of mystical happiness that overcame her in moments of great danger.

II Tasker Jevons

Tasker Jevons (*The Belfry* in America) is about a young journalist of lower middle-class background who becomes a successful novelist, marries the daughter of a canon, and finally distinguishes himself in the war. In the opening pages of the novel, Jevons is ambitious both for fame and wealth; he sets himself goals to reach in a certain number of years, and he always succeeds within his established period. He tries to imitate the manners and speech of the middle class, but in moments of nervousness and stress he is prone to drop his h's, to use the wrong personal pronouns, and to crack his knuckles. When he falls in love with Viola Thesiger, the daughter of a canon of Canterbury Cathedral, she is rebelling against her background; and she finds the vitality of Jevons and his behavior, so different from that of the young men of her class, appealing and exciting. Viola, in an attempt to break the ties with her family and class, takes an overnight trip with Jevons to Belgium to see the belfry of the church in Bruges. Although the adventure is innocent, her family considers her compromised and is willing to let her marry Jevons. They are happy enough together except that Viola's favorite brother has refused to accept Jevons and has severed all relationship with his sister.

As Jevons becomes increasingly successful as a novelist, he indulges more and more his taste for luxury and show by buying motor cars, a yacht, and larger and more ostentatious houses. With his success, Jevons relaxes; and his lapses in manner and speech become more frequent and flagrant. This behavior begins to grate on Viola's nerves; and, when the war begins, their marriage is about to end. In the war, Jevons drives an ambulance in Belgium and distinguishes himself for his heroism. The belfry in Bruges, to which Jevons had taken Viola in the first part of the novel, suggests his essential fineness of spirit, which again emerges in his wartime activities in Belgium. On one of his trips with his ambulance, he saves the life of Viola's brother; as a result, he wins back Viola and her whole family's grateful acceptance. Presumably, Viola and her family will no longer find his manners and showiness offensive.

Much good humor exists in the novel, and Sinclair draws a vivid portrait of an endearing character in Tasker Jevons. On the whole, however, the novel seems clever and superficial. The last third of the novel, which chronicles the exploits of Jevons in wartime Belgium, strikes the reader as fantastic. The war serves as a topical "deus ex machina" that saves the Jevons' marriage, for Sinclair apparently saw one of the effects of war to be the reordering of English values and the overcoming of class prejudices. For Viola's family, the courage and the self-sacrifice that Jevons shows in the front lines more than make up for his vulgarity and lack of manners. Yet the Thesiger reconciliation with Jevons seems to be less the result of their overcoming or even recognizing their class prejudice and to be more an exception made for an individual who saved their son's life.

The character of Tasker Jevons was obviously modeled on Arnold Bennett, for he resembles Bennett in his lower middle-class origins, in his peculiarities of speech, in his setting himself a certain number of years to reach a goal, and in his love of luxury and show. The name of Sinclair's character also suggests Jacob Tonson, the pseudonym with which Bennett signed the weekly column, "Books and Persons" that he wrote for *The New Age* between 1908 and 1911. However, the facts related to the marriage of Jevons do not correspond with Bennett's; and, although Bennett did tour the front lines in France, he did not take part in any heroic exploits. Bennett must have been surprised to see all his minor shortcomings delineated in a novel by a woman about whom, when he had met her in 1911, he had recorded in his journal, "I rather liked this prim virgin. Great sense."[13]

In her satirical portrait of Bennett, Sinclair may have been motivated by personal pique. In his column, Bennett had carried on a feud with William Robertson Nicoll, the editor of the *Bookman* and the *British Weekly*, by poking fun at him in issue after issue in a rather breezy supercilious manner. Nicoll had helped Sinclair when she was an unknown beginner in London by giving her reviews to do for the *Bookman* and by publishing in 1898 an article about her works in the *Bookman;* except for review notices of her first novel, this article was the first about her to appear. Another target of Bennett's in "Books and Persons" was Henry James, Sinclair's favorite among the modern novelists. Moreover, Bennett was also in the habit of denigrating women writers; for, as he stated in one column, "With the possible exception of Jane Austen and E. B. Browning, no woman has yet written a first-class novel."[14]

In 1909, in two articles about the "comfortable middle class," which, according to Bennett, formed the backbone of the novelist's reading public, he included May Sinclair in the list of inferior novelists who catered to this class by avoiding unpleasant subjects and by not upsetting their reader's belief in the status quo. He noted that the best novelists, "novelists who impressed themselves on the handful of persons whose taste is severe and sure," do not write about this class; and he listed among these best novelists, in addition to Hardy and Joseph Conrad, Wells, Rudyard Kipling, James Barrie, Eden Phillpots, W. W. Jacobs, and Murray Gilchrist. He added that the novelists who do occupy themselves with the "comfortable middle class" "are writers of the calibre of Anthony Hope, E. F. Benson, Mrs. Humphry Ward and May Sinclair. . . . Rather hard on the class that alone has made novel writing a profession in which a man can make a reasonable living."[15]

In articles like these, Bennett showed himself not above class prejudice and class envy; therefore, Sinclair aptly modeled the protagonist in a novel about English class prejudices on Bennett who referred to his "profound and instinctive hostility to this class."

However, he also revealed a somewhat ambivalent attitude to the "comfortable middle class" when he wrote, "I was born slightly beneath it. But . . . I have gained the right of entrance into it. I admit I have imitated its deportment, with certain modifications of my own. . . . I frequent it but little." Bennett also stigmatized that class for having as its chief characteristic a "religious worship of money and financial success" — values to which Bennett himself was not indifferent.[16] Sinclair obviously disagreed with Bennett's assessment of the middle-class's characteristics, since the middle-class Thesigers in her novel find Jevon's show of wealth to be vulgar and offensive and since Viola thinks her class lacks vitality and imagination. Sinclair shows in the novel that an undue regard for class distinctions victimizes all classes: the Thesigers are blinded by their class prejudice to the true character of Jevons; and Jevons, in trying to compensate for his "inferiority," wastes his energy and resources in such schemes as building an exact replica of a Tudor mansion for his home.

The novel did not create any permanent ill will between Bennett and Sinclair. In 1927, Bennett recorded in his journal that he was pleased to see and talk to Sinclair at a meeting of P. E. N.[17] To an interviewer's question, Sinclair replied that Tasker Jevons was not based on Bennett.[18] Perhaps Bennett took some comfort in the fact that Jevons is drawn in the novel as superior to his middle-class detractors in all things that really matter; a spirited and essentially good-hearted man, his enjoyment of his wealth and success is disarmingly innocent and childlike.

III · The Tree of Heaven

The Tree of Heaven (1917) is a more ambitious and more thoughtful novel than *Tasker Jevons;* for, by following the life of an English family from 1895 to 1916, Sinclair draws a broad social history of England during this period. In the first section entitled "Peace," she shows through the family of Anthony Harrison the security, prosperity, and complacency of the middle class in late Victorian and Edwardian times. In a typical scene, Mrs. Harrison serves tea to her guests in the spacious garden of her house dominated by the tree that her husband calls "an ash tree" but that Mrs. Harrison insists is a "tree of heaven." The tree of heaven is a symbol of the family's security and of an almost divine grace that seems to favor its members, since the social problems of the time touch their lives so peripherally that they hardly seem to exist.

Although Mrs. Harrison skims the pages of the *Times* every day, she considers the affairs of the nation dull and unimportant in comparison to the events in her own family. Her husband's employees might strike, but his business is so prosperous that a strike would be a minor inconvenience. When the Boer War breaks out and Mrs. Harrison's black sheep brother enlists, the family sees the war as a convenient way of putting him out of sight for a few years. The only unhappiness in Mrs. Harrison's life is caused by the presence of her three maiden sisters, now in their forties; they are obviously lonely, frustrated, and repressed; they lead empty and futile lives; and they bear the scorn and gibes of their elderly sharp-tongued mother. Mrs. Harrison does her duty by having them for tea twice a week when she is gracious to them for an hour or so and is always relieved to see them go home.

The second part of the novel, entitled "Vortex," chronicles the years 1910 to 1914, which Sinclair regards as a period of developing unrest, discord, and change. The spirit of the times is like a vortex — a force for change that sweeps people along and masters them — and the four Harrison children are affected by it. Dorothy, a recent graduate of Newnham, is active in the suffragette movement; and, because of her part in a deputation to the House of Commons, one which became violent when the police tried to interfere, she spends four weeks in jail. Her eldest brother Michael, a young poet who has refused to enter the family business, frequents the Friday night sessions of a group of writers, painters, and sculptors who propound imagist and vorticist ideas. Morton Ellis, the leader of the group, believes that poets must make a clean sweep of literary traditions by experimenting with new forms; but some of his more extreme followers believe in violence as a means of releasing creative energy. The forces of change and discord also overtake the second Harrison son, Nicholas; he leaves the university, works with his hands as an inventor-engineer, and perfects his model of the "moving-fortress," the forerunner of the tank. He marries the pregnant cast-off mistress of another man, a woman who has applied the slogan "freedom for women" to her sex life. The Harrison parents are baffled and perturbed by all these disturbing forces at work in their children's lives.

In the last section "Victory," war overtakes the family; and the previous restlessness and discord of the younger generation, as well as the selfish complacency of the older, are replaced by a spirit of harmony and self-sacrifice as all draw together in an effort to serve their country. Mrs. Harrison now places her country's interests ahead of her family's and is happy to see her sons go to the war. When Dorothy's fiancé is killed, she realizes how silly she was to have let their difference of opinion on the subject of woman's suffrage keep them apart. Michael, the young poet, as an individualist who has always kept his distance from the crowd, distrusts and abhors the kind of mass feeling that the war seems to have created. After his younger brother is killed, Michael enlists out of a sense of loyalty to his brother's memory and also dies. To his surprise, Michael experiences, like his brother, a sense of ecstasy and of the closeness of God in moments of great danger. The war brings even the children's old spinster aunts a sense of fulfillment: knitting socks and rolling bandages, they feel for the first time in their lives both needed and useful. The novel ends with the third and youngest Harrison boy, in khaki for the first time, going out of the front gate of his house on his way to war.

The Tree of Heaven was a best-seller in 1918, for it reflected the patriotic enthusiasm of the Anglo-American world.[19] The letters Michael sends to his family from the front include such phrases as the "most glorious Army in history"[20] as well as descriptions of the spiritual ecstasy that comes in moments of danger, the feeling when the possibility of death is so close that "you lay hold on eternal life."[21] Through Michael and Nicholas, Sinclair was trying to give a view of war different from that of Barbusse in Under Fire. Although she does not refer to Barbusse by name, Michael writes in one letter, "There's a Frenchman who has told the truth, piling up all the horrors, faithfully, remorselessly, magnificently" to show up the infamy of war as a deterrant, so no government will ever start another one.[22] But Michael believes that Barbusse is not likely to frighten the Germans and that, although the horrors Barbusse describes so well are a part of war, another truth about war is "our glory, our spiritual compensation for the physical torture and there would be a sort of infamy in trying to take it from us."[23] Today's reader is likely to be more in sympathy with Barbusse's view of war and to find much of this section of Sinclair's novel sentimental and unconvincing. The title "Victory" for this section, in which the two Harrison boys are killed and the third is perhaps on his way to the same fate, is meant to refer to the "spiritual compensation" Michael writes about in his letter. But, in this more skeptical age, the use of such phrases over dead bodies seems at best empty rhetoric.

The first two sections of the novel, "Peace" and "Vortex," are the best parts. The depiction of the life of the Harrison family in the first section reminds one of E. M. Forster's *Marianne Thornton* in the sense that, like Forster, Sinclair captures something of the spirit of Victorian family life — the family as creating its own self-sufficient world, the intense relationships within it, the sense of security and emotional richness. With the three maiden aunts and the drunkard uncle, Sinclair shows the converse of that world — the sense of futility and worthlessness of those excluded from the magic circle. Figures of frustration and bitterness, the three spinster aunts who weave in and out of the novel comprise one of the best creations in the novel.

The second section, "Vortex," contains some interesting social history. Indeed, Roger Fulford in *Votes for Women*, his book about the suffrage movement, quotes at length from it, especially the scene of the dinner at a hotel that was given to honor the women who had just been released from prison. Through Dorothy, Sinclair presents what were probably her own and other intelligent women's views of the Women's Social and Political Union: Dorothy works for the Union but does not join because she is critical of some of the practices of its leaders, including Mrs. Blathwaite and Angela Blathwaite, who were perhaps modeled on Mrs. Pankhurst and Christabel Pankhurst; Dorothy objects to their mindless rhetoric and to their demand for unquestioned obedience from their members.

Sinclair's description of the group of young artists that Michael meets also provides an interesting glimpse of some of the famous artists and writers in prewar England. Lawrence Stephen bears many resemblances to William Butler Yeats; and, in the prewar years before his greatest poetry was published, Sinclair saw him as sad and unfulfilled — as a man who has tried his hand at many things, Irish nationalism, politics, the theater, and poetry, but has not been a great success at any of them. He is respected but patronized by the young poet Morton Ellis, who joshes the older man for his old-fashioned tastes in poetry and who calls him a bigot for liking Swinburne.

Morton Ellis, the leader of the younger poets, resembles Ezra Pound, who had acted as Yeats's secretary, who was indeed given to patronizing him, and who once "corrected" some of Yeats's poems before mailing them to a journal. Morton Ellis preaches a doctrine of making a clean sweep of literary traditions; but, in his own poetry, Sinclair notes with amusement, he imitated "every poetic form under the sun except the forms adopted by his contemporaries."[24] Whereas Morton Ellis favors violence as a means of making a break with the past, the young painter, Austen Mitchell (Wyndham Lewis, perhaps) thinks violence is right as an end in itself because it releases creative energy.

A third artist in the group, Paul Monier-Owen, is clearly Henri Gaudier-Brzeska, the marvelously gifted young sculptor who was killed in the war in 1915. One has only to look at the photographs of Gaudier-Brzeska in Pound's book about him to be struck by the aptness of Sinclair's description of him as Monier-Owen:

> A light darted from the corner of the room where Paul Monier-Owen had curled himself up. His eyes flashed like the eyes of a young wild animal roused in its lair.
> Paul Monier-Owen was dark, soft and supple. At a little distance he had the clumsy grace and velvet innocence of a black panther, half cub, half grown. The tips of his ears, the corners of his prominent eyes, his eyebrows and his long nostrils tilted slightly upwards and backwards. Under his slender mournful nose his restless smile showed the white teeth of a young animal.
> Above this primitive savage base of features that responded incessantly to any childish provokation, the intelligence of Monier-Owen watched in his calm and beautiful forehead and in his eyes.[25]

When Sinclair wrote this passage, Gaudier-Brzeska was already dead; and her sorrow for his untimely death appears in her evocation of his vitality, youth, and intelligence.

With these characters, Sinclair touches on the relationship of the imagist group to contemporary French poetry. Lawrence Stephen gives Michael a letter of introduction to a young French poet, Jules Réveillaud; Michael discovers that, independently and without realizing it, he has been trying to do the same kind of thing in his poems as Réveillaud. Réveillaud talks to Michael about the need to experiment in poetry, to aim for *dureté* ("hardness"), and to imitate sculpture rather than painting or music.[26] In her portrayal of Réveillaud, Sinclair may have had in mind Rémy de Gourmont, whom the English imagist poets admired and whose theories her fictional character echoes.[27]

Although Sinclair portrayed the young artists of the imagist and vorticist group sympathetically, communicating their healthy vitality and their wholehearted commitment to their art, she also expressed through Michael her dislike of their herd instinct and also of their violence in personal relations.[28] For the same reasons, Sinclair's

Dorothy criticizes the suffrage movement. Although Sinclair worked for both groups, she believed too much in the independence and in the integrity of the private, unique self to approve some of their methods.

One of the reviewers of this novel indicated that the words "hard" and "clear," attributes that the imagist poets aimed for in their poetry, recur repeatedly in the novel;[29] Sinclair used not only these words but also their opposites, the favorite pejoratives of the imagists, "soft," "blurred," "fluffy," and "sentimental" to describe her characters' appearance, their emotions, and their lines of poetry. The influence of imagist principles is evident in individual scenes which are rendered by means of a collection of related images. For example, the parade after the release of the suffragettes from prison is described in terms of images that suggest the excitement, the colorfulness, and the vitality of that movement. The scene of the family's having tea under the tree of heaven in the first part of the novel, as well as the image of the vortex which dominates the second part, are perhaps examples of Sinclair's use of imagist techniques.

On the whole, this conventionally written novel has its chief interest in the narrative of events rather than in the rendering of discontinuous impressions in terms of images. Indeed, one can apply to the third part of the novel all the favorite pejorative terms of the imagists, "soft," "sentimental," and "blurred." Some evidence of the haste with which this novel was written lies in the fact that one of the characters, Morton Ellis, is said to be fighting for his country on one page and about twenty pages later is reported to have refused to do so.[30] One has the impression that Sinclair sacrificed the usual meticulous care with which she wrote and perhaps some of her artistic conscience to her eagerness to buoy up her countrymen's courage.

Wyndham Lewis summed up the spirit of the years immediately preceding the war as "one big bloodless brawl, prior to the Great Bloodletting."[31] Sinclair in the section "Vortex" captures this spirit of unrest and violence in the suffrage movement, in artistic circles, and in personal relationships. She was equally effective in the previous section in evoking the security and complacency of the late Victorian and Edwardian world. Characteristically, however, the most influential reviewers praised the last section about the war; for example, the reviewer in the *Times Literary Supplement* wrote, "Then comes the war and here Miss Sinclair's imagination works at its finest and fullest."[32] The appeal of this section of the novel probably made this her most widely read novel after *The Divine Fire*.

Two years after its appearance, Sinclair linked *The Tree of Heaven* with *The Divine Fire* as novels that gave the reviewers too many bad reasons for liking them.[33] Although one cannot be certain what she meant by this statement, she may have grown critical of this novel as her attitude toward the war became less enthusiastic. As is evident from the novels that followed it, her belief that the war was inaugurating a new era of selfless cooperation among all classes of English society did not long survive the armistice; for in these later novels she showed an awareness of increasing class hostilities.

In three novels Sinclair wrote between 1920 and 1923, she took as her protagonists members of the English ruling class and showed them to be emasculated and fearful of the working class; and she obviously no longer regarded the war as glorious. In her novels, she wrote about returning shell-shocked soldiers who were rejected by their families and about petty squabbles in the village about where to put the memorial to the war dead. In 1920, in *The Romantic*, she created as her protagonist a young man, the son of an automobile manufacturer, who romanticizes war as a compensation for his impotence. In the *Journal*, some of her impressions suggest that she was aware of a connection between sex instincts and war enthusiasm. Sinclair, who had written about the sexual overtones of St. Theresa's mystical writings in *A Defence of Idealism*, could not have been unaware of the fact that some of her own descriptions of the "spiritual ecstasy" that was experienced by men who were close to danger in the front lines had similar sexual overtones. Indeed, in *The Tree of Heaven* she has Nicholas describing the ecstasy of war in one of his letters home and arguing that it is not of a sexual nature. By 1920 in *The Romantic* and in 1921 to a lesser extent in *Mr. Waddington of Wyck*, Sinclair was suggesting that the war not only had engaged but had been a means of expressing the repressed sexual feelings of an emasculated class. However, by 1924 her optimism about England's future seemed to reassert itself; she had great hopes for the first Labour government of Ramsey MacDonald and referred to it as a "splendid experiment."[34]

CHAPTER 6

Mary Olivier: A Life

AFTER the armistice in 1918, Sinclair was freed from the burden of propagandizing the war; and, perhaps in reaction against the public voice with which she had spoken in *The Tree of Heaven*, she wrote, in 1919, *Mary Olivier: A Life*, her most subjective and her most private novel, as well as one in which, in comparison to *The Tree of Heaven*, she was more concerned with technique, more the conscious artist. Like Dorothy Richardson's *Pilgrimage*, three volumes of which had appeared by 1919, *Mary Olivier* is a stream-of-consciousness novel written in an imagist style. Sinclair considered the techniques of both imagism and the stream-of-consciousness to be attempts to capture reality; and perhaps an attempt to capture or to get closer to reality was the major concern of English novelists during the first quarter of this century. At first, naturalism was used to get at reality; but with the realization that naturalism did not fully succeed in doing so, the experimentation with the new techniques began. (One sees the dissatisfaction with naturalistic and realistic techniques in James's criticism of the work of Wells and Gissing and in Woolf's criticism of Bennett.)

I *On Imagism and the Stream of Consciousness*

Sinclair explained and defended imagism in an article which appeared in the June, 1915, issue of *The Egoist*. She began by pointing out that it is easier to specify what imagism is not rather than to state what it is — she made clear that imagism is not either imagery or symbolism. When she ventured her definition, she wrote that the image "may be the form of a thing . . . or the form of a passion, emotion, or mood. The point is that the passion, the emotion or the mood is never given as an abstraction. . . . You cannot distinguish between the thing and its image. You can, I suppose, distinguish between the emotion and its image, but only as you distinguish between sub-

stance and its form. What the imagists are 'out for' is direct naked
contact with reality."[1]

Sinclair was repeating and rephrasing some of the concepts that
had been evolved and stated by T. E. Hulme and Ezra Pound. For
example, in writing of the imagists' making "direct contact with
reality," Sinclair was echoing the imagists' belief that the image was
a moment of revealed truth. Scholars, who have indicated that the
theory of the image was a means of transcending the subject-object
dichotomy of nineteenth-century poetic theory, have cited as
evidence Hulme's indebtedness to Bergson's theory of the image
and Pound's definition of the image as "that which presents an intellectual and emotional complex in an instant of time."[2] Sinclair
was probably expressing and rephrasing the imagists' attempt to
fuse subject and object when she wrote that the image "may be the
form of a thing . . . or the form of a passion emotion or mood" in
which the image and its object are indistinguishable except as one
would distinguish between substance and form.

In an article on the poetry of F. S. Flint, she wrote that the aim of
the imagists is "to restore the innocence of memory as Gauguin
restored the innocence of the eye."[3] In this statement, Sinclair was
perhaps echoing Hulme's comparison between modern painting and
the new poetry: "What has found expression in painting as im-
pressionism will soon find expression in poetry as free verse."[4]
Sinclair believed that the imagist poet was trying to remove all
traces of himself from the poem by rendering and not commenting,
and by presenting things and emotions in themselves and not as
aspects of his reflection. She was perhaps developing the
philosophical implications of the imagist principle, "direct treatment of the 'thing' whether subjective or objective,"[5] when she
wrote that "The poet has beome what Schopenhauer called 'der rein
anschauende Subject,' the pure perceiver."[6] She saw in the writers of
the stream-of-consciousness novel the same attempt to get closer to
reality, to recapture the innocence of memory, and to become as far
as possible the pure perceiver by doing away with the interferences
of the author's comments and with the imposed and distorting structures of traditional character and plot.

Many critics have described the stream-of-consciousness novel, especially Richardson's *Pilgrimage*, as imagistic because, as in imagist
poetry, life is rendered not in terms of story or dramatic characterization, nor in terms of abstract thought and sentiment, but in terms of
impressions or concrete images.[7] As one critic stated in referring to

Pilgrimage as an imagist novel, "Miriam sees the world as a stream of sensed pictures."[8] Sinclair, in writing about imagist poetry and the stream-of-consciousness novel, went beyond noting that both techniques used concrete images and stressed the similarity of their aims.

In an article about *Pilgrimage*, Sinclair admired Richardson's stream-of-consciousness technique and noted its superiority to the "objective" method in the immediacy and the reality of its effect: "What we used to call the 'objective' method is a method of after-thought, of spectacular reflection. What has happened [Mrs. Henderson's suicide] has happened in Miriam's bedroom, if you like; but only by reflection. The first-hand, intimate and intense reality of the happening is in Miriam's mind, and by presenting it thus and not otherwise Miss Richardson seizes reality alive."[9] Sinclair may have been echoing and applying to the novel Hulme's statement that modern art was different from the art of the past in that "it no longer deals with heroic action, it has become definitely and finally introspective." He explained that the "mystery of things" was no longer perceived as "action" but as "impression."[10]

Sinclair's association with the imagist movement prepared her to respond sympathetically and perceptively to the stream-of-consciousness novel. For just as the imagist poets had dropped meter, metaphor, and abstract statement, Dorothy Richardson had dropped the traditional author's discursive comments about the material and the conventional structuring forms of the novel, such as plot and objective characterization. Sinclair thought that thereby both imagist poetry and Richardson's novel had gained in concen-tration, reality, and immediacy. The absence of traditional structures of the novel did not mean that *Pilgrimage* was formless, as some critics had complained, but that it was an attempt to impose a new kind of form:

To me these three novels show an art and method and form carried to punc-tilious perfection. Yet I have heard other novelists say that they have no art and no method and no form, and that it is this formlessness which annoys them. They say they have no beginning and no middle and no end, and that to have form a novel must have an end and a beginning and a middle. . . . In this series there is no drama, no situation, no set scene. Nothing happens. It is just life going on and on. It is Miriam Henderson's stream of consciousness going on and on. And in neither is there any discernible beginning or middle or end.

In identifying herself with this life, which is Miriam's stream of consciousness, Miss Richardson produces her effect of being the first, of getting closer to reality than any of our novelists who are trying so desperately to get close. No attitude or gesture of her own is allowed to come between her and her effect.[11]

In this article Sinclair seems to be applying to the novel many of the concepts of imagist poetry. There is "no beginning and no middle and no end" because this novel, like an imagist poem, is not a logical structure of consecutive events or thoughts but moments of intuited truth. The "objective" method is the artificial method for the firsthand reality is where subject and object are fused in Miriam's stream of consciousness, just as in the image subject and object are fused.

As early as 1918, Sinclair was not only aware of the direction the novel was taking but helped create the critical vocabulary to deal with it. She was the first to apply William James's term, "stream of consciousness," to the novel. She urged dropping the terminology of "realism and idealism" and of "subjective and objective" in art, for this terminology is "missing the new trend of the philosophies of the twentieth century. All that we know of reality at first hand is given to us through contacts in which these interesting distinctions are lost. Reality is thick and deep, too thick and too deep, and at the same time too fluid to cut with any convenient carving knife. The novelist who would be close to reality must confine himself to this knowledge at first hand. He must, as Mr. Beresford says, simply 'plunge' in."[12]

As Walter Allen has written, Virginia Woolf was indebted to this article for her own essay on the modern novel which appeared a year later.[13] In this essay Woolf seemed to follow Sinclair's lead in using the same passage in William James's *Principles of Psychology* from which Sinclair had culled the phrase "stream of consciousness." Woolf had some good words for Joyce's novels, but she criticized the novels of Arnold Bennett from which, she wrote, "life escapes." "Life is not a series of gig lamps symmetrically arranged; but a luminous halo, a semi-transparent envelope surrounding us from the beginning of consciousness to the end."[14] As Jacob Isaacs has indicated, Woolf's definition of life and her use of the phrase "luminous halo" seem to echo James's words, for James wrote that "Every definite image in the mind is steeped and dyed in the free water that flows round it. The significance, the value of the image is all in this halo or penumbra that surrounds and escorts it. . . . Consciousness does not appear to itself chopped up in bits. . . . It is nothing jointed; it flows. . . . Let us call it the stream of thought, of consciousness, or of subjective life."[15]

After Sinclair had pointed out that, according to the philosophies of the twentieth century, reality is "too fluid to cut with any convenient carving knife," she stated that, to do justice to this fluid reality, the novelist must not, just as Dorothy Richardson does not, "tell a story or handle a situation or set a scene; she must avoid drama as she avoids narration. . . . She is not concerned, in the way that other novelists are concerned, with character."[16] Woolf seemed to echo Sinclair's words when, in the passage in which she wrote of the luminous atomistic quality of life, she added that ideally in the novel there should be "no plot, no comedy, no tragedy, no love interest or catastrophe in the accepted style. . . ."[17] At one point, Woolf apologized for the vagueness of the term "life" in her phrase "life escapes," but she added, "one can scarcely better the matter by speaking, as critics are prone to do, of reality."[18]

In addition to explicating the technique of Richardson's *Pilgrimage*, Sinclair also noted some literary antecedents that had contributed to the new tendency in fiction: "I too thought, like Mr. Beresford, that Miss Richardson has been the first to plunge. But it seems to me rather that she has followed independently, perhaps unconsciously, a growing tendency to plunge. As far back as the eighties the de Goncourts plunged completely, finally, in *Soer Philomène, Germinie Lacerteux*, and *Les Frères Zemgann*. . . . Miss Richardson has not plunged deeper than James Joyce in his *Portrait of the Artist as a Young Man*."[19] By citing the de Goncourts in connection with the stream-of-consciousness novel, Sinclair was suggesting the part played by the recent psychological theories in the development of the modern novel. Although the de Goncourts were considered leaders of the naturalistic movement in France, they also were interested in and had been influenced by the works of psychologists such as Jean-Martin Charcot. In their novels, they often delved into the subjective psychological state of their characters; and, in their depiction of dreams and repressions, they suggested the existence of the unconscious.[20]

II *Stream of Consciousness in* Mary Olivier

Mary Olivier is a *bildungsroman* (a formation novel) that traces the life from infancy to middle age of a woman who attempts to form and preserve her individuality in the face of the opposition of her family and their religion. As in *The Three Sisters*, the main concern is with the mind and its impulses and feelings; however, these are not dramatized and expressed in action in *Mary Olivier*, for Sinclair adopted Richardson's method and showed the mind in its process.

As in previous novels, Sinclair criticized the institutions of family and religion and saw some human relationships in psychoanalytic terms of dependence and love-hate. But these themes as expressed through the mind of Mary Olivier have an immediacy and a particularity that take them out of the realm of ideas. For example, Mary reads the Thirty-Nine Articles (to which members of the Church of England must subscribe) against her wishes and at her mother's insistence:

> "Don't look like that," her mother said, "as if your wits were wool-gathering."
> "Wool?" She could see herself smiling at her mother disagreeably.
> Wool-gathering. Gathering wool. The room was full of wool; wool flying about; hanging in the air and choking you. Clogging your mind. Old grey wool out of pew cushions that people had sat on for centuries, full of dirt.
> Wool, spun out, wound round you, woven in a net. You were tangled and strangled in a net of unclean wool.[21]

By using the stream-of-consciousness method, Sinclair enables the reader to experience Mary Olivier's feeling of being smothered by the religion her mother forces on her. Religion becomes associated in her mind, through the word "wool," with dirt, age, and with a feeling of being strangled and trapped in a net. As Mary grows older, her impressions become more complicated and ironic; an example is Mary's spending a dull and disagreeable Sunday at school:

> The soiled light; odours from the warm roots of girl's hair; and Sunday. Sunday; stale odours of churches. You wrote out the sermon you had not listened to and had not heard. Somebody told you the text, and you amused yourself by seeing how near you could get to what you would have heard if you had listened. After tea, hymns; then church again. Your heart laboured with the strain of kneeling, arms lifted up to the high pew ledge. You breathed pew dust. Your brain swayed like a bladder, brittle, swollen with hot gas-fumes. After supper, prayers again. Sunday was over.[22]

In passages such as these, one feels that Sinclair communicated her anti-religious sentiments through poetry rather than through ideas. These passages also show that Sinclair applied in this novel some of the dicta of imagism that she mentioned in her article — that "there must be nothing between you and your object" and that "emotion or mood is never given as an abstraction."

Although the two passages quoted have the disconnected quality of sense impressions and thoughts in process, they are, indeed, carefully selected by the author to communicate a certain attitude and experience of the character. Sinclair gives the stream of consciousness directly only in some passages, as in the paragraph beginning "Wool gathering. Gathering wool. The room was full of wool;" In other passages Mary reports her thoughts and impressions in the second person as in "You breathed pew dust. Your brain swelled like a bladder." When Mary moves further away from the stream of her own thoughts, she observes herself as a third person and uses the third person pronoun. Indeed through much of the novel the reader is not aware of Mary's consciousness in process, for Mary acts as the narrator reporting in conventional third person declarative sentences her impressions and observations in consecutive time without the play of her memory or her subjective thought. The result is more coherence and a greater sense of movement than in Richardson's novel, but not as great an effect of "plunging."

III *Criticism of Victorian Values*

The theme of the stultifying effect of religion runs through much of the novel. Religion is used, especially by Mary's mother, as an instrument of punishment and domination. As a little girl, Mary longs for her mother's affection and approval; but her mother, under the pretext of teaching her daughter the religious virtues of humility and selflessness, is critical and cold. In the battles between mother and daughter over religion, Mary is fighting for her individuality and her mother is struggling for dominion over her daughter.

The values of obedience and humility the parents try to instill in the children are seen as being destructive. For a long time Mary is denied the books she longs for because her mother believes that such a desire in a girl is a sign of willfullness and arrogance. On the whole, the children's desires and abilities are not considered. Roddy, who has a weak heart, is made a farmer and dies of a heart attack; another son, who loves animals, is put to work in an office.

The relationships between parents and children are depicted by Sinclair in psychoanalytic terms of the love-hate that destroys the idea of the "holy family." The mother, disillusioned by her husband, prefers her sons, especially the eldest, Mark; and she looks upon Mary as a rival for his affections. The father, who in turn hates his sons for being preferred by his wife, is cruel to them and at times is pathetically docile to his wife. When he wants to get back at her, he is particularly affectionate to Mary. None of the boys marries, for their attachment to their mother is too strong. Mary also is caught in a love-hate relationship with her mother, which she does not completely understand. Though Mary realizes her mother is jealous of her and at times hates her, she continues to long for the acceptance and affection her mother denies her. The reader is left to infer that Mary's father is such a weak and pathetic figure that Mary's love for him has been diverted to her mother. In later years, Mary falls in love and has an affair but refuses to marry because she feels she cannot leave her now senile and invalid mother.

The love-hate relationships in Mary's family are the continuation in the second and third generation of the problems that had existed in her grandparent's family. Mary's father Emilius grew up in a family in which his youngest sister, Charlotte, was the favorite child and for whom the parents expected the other children to make sacrifices. Charlotte, once the overprotected and overindulged baby of the family, is fortyish, unmarried, and hysterical. Her hysteria takes the form of fantasizing a romance with any man she meets, of writing love letters, and of setting dates for her weddings to men who are scarcely aware of her existence. Her family, scandalized by her behavior, try isolating her from men and from society; but this attempt only aggravates her condition. Charlotte keeps little dolls, her babies she calls them, which she gives away to her young niece Mary whenever she convinces herself she is about to be married. They are symbols of the frustration of her wasted life that she willingly parts with when she feels she is about to escape.

Charlotte's mother has made Victor and Lavinia, her two older children, promise that they would take care of Charlotte and never institutionalize her. Victor lives his life as the guardian and manager of his sister and Lavinia as her nurse. Lavinia, as an unmarried dependent sister in her brother's house, is not even allowed the right to her own opinions; and she must practice her one outlet of religious worship surreptitiously because her brothers disapprove of her religious nonconformity. At this time, Lavinia is thirty-three and still has the spark of an independent spirit; but, by the end of the novel, her years of dependency and emptiness have left her a tired shell of a woman who vaguely prattles about God's love.

Victor fares no better than his sisters. He refuses to marry because he is afraid of passing on to his children Charlotte's insanity. After he is forced to institutionalize his increasingly violent sister, he falls or jumps out of the window of the room in which Charlotte had been closeted. Emilius, Mary's father, unable to get from his wife the affection he craves, gradually takes to drink. While Emilius's drinking is becoming a serious problem, Mary's mother pretends it does not exist because to admit his problem would be too mortifying to her vanity and sense of respectability. Likewise, in part, a sense of respectability had made Charlotte's mother demand that her other children take care of Charlotte instead of institutionalizing her.

The older generation and their problems are kept in the background; for, as a young girl, Mary has only vague glimmerings of their existence. But, as she grows older and begins to feel the burden of her own narrow and empty life as the manager of the household in a dull provincial town, the fate of Lavinia and Charlotte is always present to her mind, and she begins to fear that her fate will be the same. Like any young girl, Mary becomes interested successively in a number of young men; but her mother does everything she can to discourage these romances, partly because she wants to keep her only daughter bound to her, partly because she wants to teach her daughter humility, and partly because she sees Mary as a rival for the affections of her favorite son Mark and hence is jealous of her. More than once she hints to Mary that she is only fantasizing that these young men are interested in her, that she is just like her Aunt Charlotte in this respect.

As Mary grows older and continues her dull life, she feels more keenly the frustration of her empty life: "To you nothing happened. Nothing would ever happen. At twenty-one and a half you were old too, and very wise. You had given up expecting things to happen. You put 1883 on your letters to Mark and Dan and Roddy, instead of 1882. Then 1884. You measured time by the books you read and by the poems you wrote. . . ."[23] Later she muses, "You would be like Aunt Lavvy. You would live in Morfe with Mamma for years and years as Aunt Lavvy had lived with Grandmamma. . . . No; when you were forty-five you would go like Aunt Charlotte."[24] "Suddenly you would go smash. Smash. Your mind would die in a delirium of hunger."[25] In these moods, she sees herself as her Aunt Lavinia, as a daughter sacrificed to her mother's sense of propriety and obedience until, like her Aunt Charlotte, she goes mad. As Mary's situation indicates, the family, far from being holy, is destructive to its members; it is a trap that, through ties of affection and the weapons of religion and of conventional respectability and propriety, demands of its members unconditional surrender.

IV A Biography of the "New Woman"

The unifying theme of the novel is Mary's struggle to free herself from her family and from sharing the fate of Lavinia and Charlotte, to express her own individuality, and to find her own standards as alternatives to those of religious conformity and conventional propriety that rule her family. Mary Olivier is, in short, the new woman who is trying to free herself from past tradition, to express her own selfhood, and to live by her own standards. From adolescence on, Mary Olivier is engaged in this struggle from which she emerges alternately successful and defeated. At fourteen, she wages a successful battle against her mother over her right to read her brother's books. She also wages a battle with her mother over religion because she finds her parents' religion repressive and life denying and because she longs to know a God more real and more satisfying to her moral sense. She reads Spinoza, Kant, and Hegel; and she is dazzled for a while by Spinoza's God. Fearing at times that she is determined by her heredity and circumstances to become like her aunts Charlotte and Lavinia, she reads all the books she can find about heredity — Charles Darwin, Henry Maudsley, Théodule A. Ribot, and Ernst Haeckel. Her rejection of her parents' religion and her fears about her own destiny lead her to a metaphysical quest about the nature of God and about the question of freedom and determinism in human life.

At certain times in her life, Mary feels that she has escaped the dominance of her family; for, in reading books, in writing poems, and in enjoying the beauty of nature Mary manages to maintain a life for herself apart from her mother and her household duties. At other times, her life seems empty and futile to her. She dreams of looking for her favorite brother Mark, who was always particularly affectionate to her, and not finding him: "The passages led through empty and grey lit rooms to the bottom of the kitchen stairs, and she would find a dead baby lying among the boots and shoes in the cat's cupboard."[26] As a little girl, Mary was often the puzzled recipient of Charlotte's dolls, "her little babies" as Charlotte called them, which her mother would hide in the cupboard. The dead baby in Mary's dream is the symbol of her wasted life. The stairs, the empty rooms, looking for and not being able to find Mark (into whose arms as a child she would jump from the stairs), finding instead a dead baby (associated with Charlotte's madness) — all work together to suggest also Mary's sexual fears and frustrations.

When Mary is forty, she again goes through a period of upheaval and desolation; but she emerges from this crisis with a greater sense of serenity and with a feeling that she has after all escaped the fate of Lavinia and Charlotte. With this answer to her personal quest for freedom and fulfillment comes also the answer to her quest about the nature of reality and of God. The events that bring about her crisis are, first, the termination of a brief but happy love affair with a man whom she must reject because she cannot abandon her now senile and invalid mother and, second, the subsequent death of her mother. After each of these events Mary feels a sense of desolation which is followed by a sense of peace and of the mystical presence of God. By this time, Mary has become a fairly successful writer; and she feels at last that she is herself, not what her mother wanted her to be, not like Lavinia and Charlotte, but free to be herself. In art and in her mystical experiences of God Mary has found the answer to her quest. For in these experiences she feels free from the turmoil and compulsions of her past, at one with the world and with the best that is in herself.

The central theme of the novel, Mary's struggle to escape the death of her individuality and integrity, is realized through recurring imagery of greyness and death as opposed to that of light and life. The light is associated with truth and with that part of herself that is alive and that has escaped her mother's domination. Poetry, philosophy, and experiences of happiness in nature are described in terms of light and brightness. She compares going from the Christian God to Spinoza's God as moving from a dark room to a room flooded with light. After she matures, the men she falls in love with are the ones she admires for the clarity and lucidity of their minds.

In contrast, her mother's world is described in terms of greyness and death. Mary thinks of the light in church as soiled light and of trying to learn her catechism as stuffing her mind with grey wool. If light is the truth for which she longs, greyness is the muddle from which she is trying to free herself — a muddle-headedness she sees as spawned by and necessary for middle-class respectability. Mary's mother, for example, refuses to admit even to herself that first her husband and then her son have taken to drink; for such an admission would upset her belief in her family's respectability. And poor Lavinia's unitarianism cannot even be discussed in their home, for nonconformity is proper only for servants. In Mary's recurrent dream of wandering through the house looking for Mark and finding a dead child, the rooms are described as empty and grey. Mary recognizes that part of herself, the part that still longs for her mother's affection and approval, is not free; and she sees this aspect of herself as that of a dead child: "The part that cared was not free. Not free. Prisoned in her mother's bedroom with the yellow furniture that remembered. Her mother's face that remembered. Always the same vexed, disapproving, remembering face. And her own heart sinking at each beat, dragging remembrance. A dead child, remembering and returning."[27]

V *Psychoanalytic and Mystical Ideas*

Mary's struggle and reconciliation can be interpreted to a certain extent in psychoanalytic terms as a struggle for self-understanding and self-fulfillment. She comes to realize that her desire for her mother's approval is ultimately destructive to herself; for, as she observes, "To be happy with her [her mother] either you or she had to be broken, to be helpless and little as a child."[28] When she also realizes that her mother's ideal of humility and self-repression is destructive, she complains to her brother, ". . . we were brought up all wrong. Taught that ourselves were beastly, that our wills were beastly, and that everything we liked was bad. Taught to sit on our wills, to be afraid of ourselves, and not trust them for a single minute."[29]

Although Mary's repressive upbringing and love-hate relationship with her mother have hindered her, she manages through sublimation to express her energies in ideas, in art, and in mystical experiences; and she achieves in this way some measure of fulfillment and of happiness. The novel was interpreted in such a way in the *New York Medical Journal* in one of its rare reviews of novels. The reviewer saw the novel as showing how a person learns to understand himself and the forces in his life that have hindered him and so "with difficulty and through a dash for freedom can find that deep peace and power which belong to his own work and his own expression."[30] The reviewer saw the novel as manifesting the need for analysis after an age of repression.

This reviewer's interpretation is, however, only partial; for Mary's progression from childhood to maturity is depicted not only in psychoanalytic terms of self-knowledge and sublimation but also in terms of the stations of the mystic way. The novel is divided into five books — infancy, childhood, adolescence, maturity, and middle age; and, after the books on infancy and childhood, central to each of the subsequent books is one of the stages of the mystic way. In adolescence, self-awakening; in maturity, detachment and illumination; and, in middle age, the dark night of the soul and the unitive life. Sinclair's espousal of mysticism is closely related to her already discussed adherence to Green's philosophical idealism according to which man's attainment of his best self was an expression of and discovery of the divine in his own life. Mary Olivier expresses this belief when she muses ". . . the Kingdom of God was within them . . . God was their real self. Their hidden self was God."[31] Several of Green's commentators, including Sinclair, considered his philosophy to be mystical; but Sinclair had had the stations of the mystic way suggested to her by Evelyn Underhill's *Mysticism.* This book, published in 1911, was considered to be the classic work in its field; and in the preface, the author acknowledged that Sinclair had been one of the readers of her manuscript and one from whom she had received "much helpful and expert advice."[32] Sinclair, in her *A Defence of Idealism,* acknowledged Underhill's help in introducing her to some of the classics of mystical thought; and her dedication to E. S.-M. probably refers to Evelyn Stuart-Moore, Miss Underhill's married name.

Sinclair incorporated mysticism into philosophical idealism in *A Defence of Idealism* by considering mysticism to be the experience on the emotional level of philosophical monism. In this book, in which she devoted a chapter to the "new mysticism," she defended the validity of mystical experience especially in its "new" form, one which she distinguished from traditional Christian mysticism and related to Eastern mysticism by the fact that in new mysticism man's physical desires are not repressed, but accepted, valued for what they are, and worked through.

The stations of the mystic way used as a principle of progression in *Mary Olivier* are the stations identified and described by Underhill in *Mysticism.* In the book on adolescence, Mary Olivier undergoes a self-awakening to the transcendental life. The book opens with a scene in the garden when Mary feels a "sudden, secret happiness," but Mary can only account for it vaguely: "It had something to do with the trees standing up in the golden white light. It had come before with a certain sharp white light flooding the fields, flooding the room."[33] Only much later in life does Mary interpret this experience as a presence of the divine. Underhill described such an awakening to the transcendent as "the beginning of a life process, a breaking down of the old and the building up of the new"[34] and as a "struggle towards clearness of sight."[35] In Mary's case, the old consists of her family's order of reality; the new consists of the reality she finds for herself in her books, in poetry, and in her transcendent experiences in nature.

Underhill considered this intimate realization of the divine, which she called self-awakening, as being related to a realization of the "love and sorrow at the heart of things, the discord between perfect love and an imperfect world."[36] Mary's perception of the sorrow at the heart of things and of the imperfections of human love occur in two climactic and traumatic experiences when she witnesses her Aunt Charlotte going berserk and being violently dragged away by her brother, and again when her mother, to teach Mary humility, insists that Mary was expelled from school when Mary knows, as the school officials have told her, that her mother sent for her. These two experiences mark the end of her childhood and of her belief that all is well in the world.

In the book on maturity, Mary undergoes purification and illumination. Purification, according to Underhill, involves detachment, abandonment of outward things that confine and "enchain the spirit,"[37] and mortification, "the death of the selfhood in its narrow individualistic sense"[38] and "the raising to their purest state of all that remains" by a "deliberate recourse to painful experience and difficult tasks."[39] Simply stated, detachment involves a denial of false interests, and mortification is the assertion of higher ones. Mary successively detaches herself from two young men with whom she once thought she was in love; and she then undergoes mortification by surrendering a much longed-for trip to the south of France in order to take care of her sick brother. While she is making this decision, she experiences an illumination which Underhill describes as an "exalted state of mystic consciousness in which there is a living and joyous relation between the Absolute and the self."[40] Though Mary at first feels terrible anguish at the thought of not taking her trip, she prays and then in a mystical experience her desire to go leaves her and she feels "a sense of exquisite security, clarity, and joy."[41]

In the book on middle age, Mary's feelings of desolation after she rejects her lover and after her mother dies can be likened to the dark night of the soul. But these periods of desolation are followed by a greater and richer sense of the presence of God, during which her sense of self and of time is obliterated: "She had a sense of happiness and peace suddenly with her in her room. Not so much her own as the happiness and peace of an immense, invisible, intangible being of whose life she was thus aware."[42] Through this mystic certainty come the answers to all her questions about religion, about art, and about herself and her ability to escape the fate of her aunts. In her lengthy rumination which follows, she sees this experience of mystic certainty as providing the basis for an alternative to Christianity, the basis for the value of beauty and of art, and as a vindication of her personal freedom. She now sees her early experience in the garden as her first glimmering of a transcendent reality. It should be noted that the mystic way that Mary travels is not conceived in narrowly Christian terms but as the path according to which Mary Olivier's spiritual consciousness unfolds.

Certain problems are inherent in using concepts both from psychoanalysis and mysticism to mark the stages of Mary's development and to provide the structural pattern of the novel. Mary's acts of mortification — such as the sacrifice of her longed-for trip to France to look after her brother and, later on, of her lover to look after her mother — and the spiritual exaltation that follows each of these acts of self-sacrifice seem suspect from a psychoanalytic point of view. They may seem to be vestiges of her self-repressive upbringing according to which acts of humility and self-sacrifice were exalted. Sinclair seems to have been aware of the disparity between her psychoanalytic beliefs and her belief in philosophical idealism, and she tried to mediate this disparity by considering the psychoanalytic concept of sublimation as a kind of self-sacrifice of a lower good for a higher good. But surrendering the man she loved and was happy with in order to take care of her senile mother, who now barely recognizes her, from a psychoanalytic viewpoint would probably be considered a case of Mary's denying her sexual role as a result of the confused family relationships in her childhood. From such a viewpoint Mary is still the dead child she dreamed about that longs for her mother's love.

Aside from the fact that the psychoanalytic and the mystical aspects of the novel seem at times to be at odds, the descriptions of Mary's mystical experiences and of the unitive life in the final pages of the book are too abstract, discursive, and exalted to be convincing or moving. In *The Three Sisters*, Gwenda, in much the same way as Mary Olivier, sacrifices her life to taking care of her parent; but in the 1914 novel, written before the war, no mystical reconciliation occurs that compensates for Gwenda's suffering. Although the experience of the war turned many people into skeptics, it forced Sinclair, as it did others, to more emphatic philosophical and religious beliefs. She wrote two books on philosophy during and a few years after the war and in certain passages in her letters she seems to be casting about for some way of coming to terms with some of the scenes of horror and human suffering that she had witnessed at the front.[43]

VI *Evaluation*

But the power and the effectiveness of *Mary Olivier* do not depend on the mysticism of the final pages, on its criticism of the family and religion, nor on its psychoanalytic approach. The source of the novel's power lies in its rendering of the experiences of a bright woman as she struggles for her individuality in adverse circumstances. The reader has seldom had the opportunity in the literature of that time to read and to have an inner view of what it feels like to be a woman who is not happy in the domestic role, who longs for affection and acceptance, but who clings doggedly to her determination to be herself. In comparison to Mary Olivier, characters such as H. G. Wells's Ann Veronica are pale shadows. Wells, writing in the realistic style, depicts Ann Veronica's actions, but he does not give the reader a sense of her interior life; her struggles and conflicts as a "new woman" are not explored or recreated on the level of her consciousness, but only as they issue in action.

Some of the best things in the novel are Sinclair's descriptions of the experiences of childhood and adolescence, as in the following passage about Mary's playing with her favorite brother, Mark:

Mark stood at the foot of the stairs and Mary stood at the turn. She had one hand on the rail of the banister the other pressed hard against the wall. She leaned forward on tiptoe, measuring her distance. When she looked at the stairs they fell from under her in a grey dizziness, so that Mark looked very far away.

They waited until Papa had gone back into the library — Mark held out his arms.

"Jump, Minky! Jump!"

She let go the rail and drew herself up. A delicious thrill of danger went through her and out at her fingers. She flung herself into space and Mark caught her. His body felt hard and strong as it received her. They did it again and again.

That was the "faith-jump." You knew that you would be killed if Mark didn't catch you, but you had faith that he would catch you and he always did.[44]

Mary, still childish at seventeen, becomes engaged to a man she does not love. Her fiancé, Maurice, realizing that she does not care for him, and disliking her strong will and intellectual qualities, tries to break off the engagement, giving as the reason his poverty. But Mary insists that poverty would be a petty and worldly reason for turning him away, so poor Maurice is driven to appealing to her mother to release him from the engagement. That night Mary muses:

> She didn't want him. But she wanted Somebody. Somebody. Somebody. He had left her with this ungovernable want.
> Somebody. If you lay very still and shut your eyes he would come to you. You would see him. You knew what he was like. He had Jimmy's body and Jimmy's face and Mark's ways. He had the soul of Shelley and the mind of Spinoza and Immanuel Kant.[45]

In these two passages describing Mary's doing the faith jump with Mark and her reveries about the ideal lover, Sinclair captures the emerging eroticism of the young Mary Olivier. In Mary's relationship to Maurice, Sinclair conveys Mary's absurdly high-minded and bookish qualities as well as her unrealistic expectations, all of which make her unacceptable to a conventional young man and create problems for herself. For Mary, like Gwenda, from an early age lets ideas dominate and direct her emotional life.

Many of the contemporary reviewers of *Mary Olivier* criticized the novel for what were considered at the time its offensive erotic passages. The reviewer in the *Times Literary Supplement* wrote: "The great majority of mankind are concerned primarily with preservation, but Miss Sinclair will have it that it is with generation first that we are preoccupied."[46] In Sinclair's letter to Wells, she thanked him for his letter praising her novel and lamented the response of many of her reviewers: "It is not honest to leave sex altogether out of a 'Life.' But if you put so little of it in there are people who will not see or remember anything else."[47]

In contrast to many reviewers, Katherine Mansfield in her review in *The Athenaeum* was not disturbed by its lack of reticence but by its technique: "Its aim, as we understand it, is to represent things and persons as separate, as distinct, as apart as possible."[48] She saw no connecting themes in the novel and no structure; she found in *Mary Olivier* merely a succession of surface impressions which could not accomplish the "aim of art . . . to reveal a little of the mystery of life."[49] She felt that, if this new technique were accepted, anyone could be a novelist by merely recording his surface impressions. She expressed the same misunderstanding of the stream-of-consciousness in her reviews of Dorothy Richardson, for she also considered her technique to be one that denied artistic principles of selectivity and order.

Among the more favorable comments that *Mary Olivier* received at the time were those of Richard Aldington and E. M. Forster. Aldington in an essay about Proust referred favorably to *Mary Olivier* by commenting that it could help the English reader cope with the method of Proust.[50] E. M. Forster wrote a favorable review of *Mary Olivier;* but he, like Katherine Mansfield, seemed to be somewhat puzzled by the method of narration. He called the novel a "notable experiment, unattempted hereto,"[51] but he was not very incisive as to what was new and different about it: "In the old-fashioned novels we met the heroine at 17 and left her at 18 to the sound of wedding bells. Then came realism and insisted that we should meet her in her cradle and not leave her until her death, which was generally postponed until she was a discredited grandmother. Miss Sinclair has chosen a middle course. She begins at the beginning, like the realists, but she does not go on till the end — and so she allows our imagination and sentimentality a little play after all."[52]

Forster apparently realized that the method was neither that of the Victorian novel nor that of realism, for he noted the novel's imagistic, impressionistic style: "It is built out of an immense number of details — little wedges of mosaic that are incisive rather than brilliant." He had reservations about this style which he called "both jerky and monotonous," and he found the novel "austere almost to bleakness, tart almost to acidity." One can surmise from his comments about the monotony and austerity of *Mary Olivier* that he was reacting to the novel's lack of the structured plot and the dramatic turning points in which his own novels abound. Understandably, as a humanist, he also had reservations about Mary's mystical illumination at the end of the novel. On the whole, however, he was impressed by the novel, and he called it a "moving document" and a "noble and notable experiment." He concluded, "All who care for seriousness in literature should read *Mary Olivier.*"[53]

VII   Mary Olivier *and the* Bildungsroman

The *bildungsroman*, or life novel, of which *Mary Olivier* is an example, was enjoying a vogue in England at the time. As W. C. Frierson pointed out, the Edwardian and Georgian tendency to question traditional values and to seek new values found a convenient vehicle of expression in the life novel, in which a protagonist struggled to come to terms with his society and to discover his own philosophy of life. The example of Wells's novels — *Kipps, Mr. Polly,* and *Tono-Bungay* — and the great success of Romain Rolland's *Jean Christophe,* which appeared in English between 1910 and 1913, made the life novel a favorite medium among English novelists in the second decade of the twentieth century.[54] Indeed, *Mary Olivier* bears many resemblances to *Jean Christophe* in the broad outlines of the struggle for selfhood that the child and adolescent undergoes in his family, its ambivalence toward parents, its questioning of their values, its spiritual and physical restlessness and the gradual, painful structuring of its own values.

VIII   Mary Olivier *and* Pilgrimage

As a life novel written from a woman's point of view, *Mary Olivier* closely resembles Richardson's *Pilgrimage,* with which it can most fruitfully be compared. The subject of both novels is a woman's quest for self-identity, a search that becomes at the same time one for a viable metaphysical and social reality. Central to both Miriam Henderson's and Mary Olivier's quest is a dissatisfaction with conventional religious and social ideas. In Sinclair's novel, these are primarily the Victorian values by which her family lives; in Richardson's novel, her disaffection is primarily with what she considers to be masculine ways of perceiving and acting — blind, emptily logical, and complacent. Even her distrust of Christianity comes under this category, for she views Christianity as being essentially masculine and as sharing in all the masculine faults.[55] A large part of both Mary Olivier's and Miriam Henderson's disaffection with society is a disaffection with the role women are expected to play in it. Mary Olivier's arguments with her mother over her right to read books and Miriam Henderson's diatribes against charming women both stem from this same source.

In certain respects, both novels can be considered social-problem novels; but, at the same time, both are autobiographical *bildungsromans*. Gloria Glikin has documented the autobiographical element

in *Pilgrimage;*[56] Sinclair's *Mary Olivier* is also autobiographical; and
such autobiographical elements account for some of the similarities
between the two novels since both are about individualistic and artistic women who are coming of age at the turn of the century. Both
heroines are searching for new values, and their search is marked by
sporadic feelings of guilt, ambivalence, and anxiety. Both Miriam
and Mary often feel that they are different from other women; and,
although their difference makes them feel absurd and guilty, they
doggedly pursue and cultivate their individuality. They see the old
values, the old way of life from which they are trying to escape, as essentially deadening; and both heroines operate between two
polarities — determinism, death, and madness versus freedom, life,
and happiness. Both Miriam and Mary are haunted by the fear of in-
heriting insanity, Miriam her mother's and Mary her aunt's; and
each heroine sees the insane woman as a victim of what is wrong
with society and of what each fears and wants to escape. Miriam sees
her mother as victimized by her father's limitations and by empty
religious pieties,[57] and Mary regards both aunts as victims of being
women in a world that stigmatizes their sexual urges and that
relegates the single woman to an empty life.

In Richardson's *The Tunnel*, published in the same year as *Mary
Olivier*, Miriam reiterates a number of times her fear that she "is
meant to go mad."[58] Later, she muses over her inheritance and, like
Mary, concludes, "it would bring in the end, somewhere about middle age, the state people call madness."[59] In these moods, she sees
herself as "existing merely as a link without individuality."[60] By the
end of her quest, Miriam, like Mary, feels herself delivered from her
fears. As she picks up her friend's baby, she feels "the complete still-
ing of every one of my competing urgencies. Freedom. . . . a sense of
perfect serenity."[61]

The journey, or quest, and then deliverance to freedom of Miriam
is described, as in *Mary Olivier*, both in mystical and psychological
terms. Miriam feels guilt and anxiety about her rejection of a
domestic role and also about her mother's death. When her sister
marries and she has to assume her sister's role as their mother's
nurse, she resents having to give up her own independent life. When
her mother commits suicide while Miriam has left her unattended,
she feels terrible remorse. Years later, she still feels overwhelming
guilt: "Of having brought things about, let things happen that need
not happen, one does not think. The fear of being crippled by condemnation."[62]

Gradually, her guilt subsides; and she feels it less vividly. By the end of the *Pilgrimage,* when she has experienced serenity and happiness, she muses about her deliverance: "Unforgiven we scuttle away into illusions. If one could only forgive oneself, the energy it takes to screen off the memory of the past would be set free."[63] Clearly at work in each heroine is a similar progressive, psychological process — of defiance, guilt, struggle, acceptance or reintegration, and serenity. For both Mary and Miriam the process involves the freeing of the energies required to fight the terrors and guilt of their past and the redirection of these energies into the creative channels of mystical experiences and artistic creation.

A more obvious similarity between the two works is the religious mysticism both authors use to structure their novels and to provide the answer to their heroines' quests. As Caesar Blake has shown in his book about Richardson, Miriam undergoes awakening to the transcendent in *Oberland,* purification and mortification in *Dawn's Left Hand,* and illumination in *Dimple Hill.* Her awakening in *Oberland,* like Mary Olivier's, takes the form of the experience of the transcendent in nature; her purification, her detachment from her lovers; her illumination, her felt experience of the presence of God. In both *Pilgrimage* and *Mary Olivier,* the reader feels, however, that the psychological and the mystical points of view do not always coalesce. The action of both heroines in barring themselves from young men and future husbands may seem to the reader not so much a case of purification on the mystic way, as the authors suggest, but a kind of penance that the heroines must perform to assuage their guilt about their conflicting emotions toward their mothers and about their rejection of their mothers' values. This observation may seem like an unfair piece of psychoanalyzing on the reader's part; but, on the other hand, Miriam herself, musing about her responsibility over her mother's death, thinks, "I had forfeited my share in humanity forever and must go guiltily and alone until the end."[64]

Babette Deutsch, when reviewing both *The Tunnel* and *Mary Olivier,* wrote that both novels read like a "fictional transcription of May Sinclair's *Defence of Idealism.*"[65] Indeed, both writers were committed to philosophical idealism. Miriam refers approvingly to Emerson, McTaggart, and *Robert Elsmere* a number of times; for she sees idealism with its emphasis on consciousness and its room for mysticism as a preferable alternative to masculine realism and as being more congenial to the feminine sensibility. Miriam's mysticism is also related to Quaker thought and is less transcendental and more tentative than Mary's, especially in *March Moonlight,* some of which was written as late as 1944.

When writing about Dorothy Richardson, the custom has been to emphasize her uniqueness and to attempt, at the same time, to relate her in some way to Virginia Woolf. Blake, for example, wrote, "She seems to stand apart, her novel almost *sui generis,* in her uncompromising commitment to the primacy of individual sensibility. . . . She seems to speak for no major group, nor to be significantly close intellectually to other better known writers of our time."[66] Unsuccessfully, he tried to relate her to Virginia Woolf and the Bloomsbury circle: "the body of ideals we assume to have characterized Bloomsbury would seem superficially congenial to Dorothy Richardson. But one cannot find in the composite body of beliefs embraced by the famous friends of Bloomsbury, including the ethical theories of G. E. Moore . . . a pattern for Dorothy Richardson's principles."[67]

When one considers *Pilgrimage* in the light of *Mary Olivier,* Richardson is not as unique as she may seem, and her intellectual predilections are not those of Bloomsbury and G. E. Moore but the philosophical idealism and mysticism she shared with Sinclair. Aside from their stated support of certain idealistic philosophers, both Sinclair and Richardson emphasized in their respective novels some of the leading ideas of idealistic philosophy. Both heroines implicitly and explicitly are concerned with their self-development and individuality; for both, achievement of their own individuality goes hand in hand with a discovery of the divine element in their lives; both find their greatest source of happiness in these moments of discovery and not in personal relationships; both also see these moments as answering their quest for freedom; and, finally, both novels, like the philosophy of T. H. Green, show some concern for ameliorating social conditions and can be considered, in a secondary sense, as vehicles for communicating ideas that are intended to purify middle-class values and habits of thought, particularly about women.

The idealistic philosophy shared by Richardson and Sinclair was not the philosophy of Bloomsbury or of G. E. Moore. G. E. Moore as a neorealist did not develop any metaphysical system and his ethics were personal rather than social. The highest values he recognized were personal affections and aesthetic enjoyments, and these are the values reflected in Virginia Woolf's novels. In contrast to Woolf, both Sinclair and Richardson did not consider relationships of affection as having primary value but as impediments to the realization of illuminated moments. Miriam muses: "Fully to recognize one must be alone. Away in the farthest reaches of one's being. As one can richly be with others, provided they have no claims. . . . With others on neutral territory, where one can forget one is there, and be everywhere."[68] Mary Olivier comes to the same conclusion when she says, "If you looked back on any perfect happiness you saw that it had not come from people or from the things you thought it had come from but from somewhere inside yourself. When you attached it to people they ceased for that moment to be themselves."[69]

In certain respects, however, Richardson was closer to Woolf than to Sinclair. In the volumes of *Pilgrimage* after 1919 Richardson's use of the stream-of-consciousness technique seems closer to Woolf's, from whose work she probably learned. (Seven of the thirteen volumes of *Pilgrimage* appeared after Woolf's *Jacob's Room*.) There is much greater interpenetration of perception, memory, and anticipation, a greater use of subjective time than in her earlier volumes or than in *Mary Olivier*, in which time is more objective and more consecutive. There is also in *Mary Olivier* much greater control of the stream of consciousness, whereas in *Pilgrimage* it often seems like a random selection of momentary reflections. Richardson, like Woolf, had as part of her intent the exploration of feminine sensibility for its own sake, in order to communicate the essence of feminine intuition and the unique quality of a feminine perception as opposed to masculine realism, whereas Sinclair used the stream of consciousness as a tool for gaining greater realism by giving a fuller and more real picture of her character. Sinclair did not set any particular value on feminine intuition or feminine sensibility, and her own style is more discursive, more formalistic, and more logical. Hence she missed what Richardson and Woolf provided so richly — that is, the nuances of human feeling as it is caught on the wing and the diverse elements that make up a human response to any given person or situation. Sinclair tended to be more discursive and abstract, giving greater play in her novel to both psychoanalytic and mystical ideas. At the same time she censored her heroine's stream of consciousness less and dwelt more than Richardson on the less polite and respectable human feelings. For example, Mary Olivier thinks about her feelings of hatred toward her mother and indulges in reveries about men. By using Mary Olivier's dreams, Sinclair also delves into a level of mind deeper than consciousness, in which

Mary's sexual longings and frustrations are forcefully expressed. Richardson, in the volumes published up to 1919, tended to censor the underside of human feeling, and even Miriam's feelings about her mother's suicide, "the darkest moment of my life," collectively in the thirteen volumes of *Pilgrimage* take up no more than one page.

Trying to establish cross influences between Richardson and Sinclair is a tempting but fruitless task. The only direct influence that can be established is that Sinclair was influenced by Richardson's use of the stream of consciousness. One cannot assume that Sinclair owed to Richardson's *Pilgrimage* her use of mysticism and, more specifically, of the stations of the mystic way as a structuring principle in her novel. The first three volumes of *Pilgrimage* that had appeared before *Mary Olivier* are not explicitly mystical, for they only record moments of a heightened sense of reality that only in later volumes are viewed as moments of mystical illumination. Nor can one assume that Richardson owed to Sinclair's philosophical works her interest in mysticism. Although Shiv Kumar has speculated that Richardson's interest in idealistic philosophy may have been aroused through Sinclair's *Defence of Idealism*[70] and although Babette Deutsch noted that to a degree *The Tunnel* reads like a fictional transcription of Sinclair's *Defence of Idealism*, one cannot be certain that Richardson read this work and was influenced by it. However, both authors did share a common belief in idealism and mysticism which can account for some of the similarities between the two novels. Both authors were indebted to Underhill's *Mysticism*, which Richardson described as "the boldest and clearest sighted, the most comprehensive and lucid description of the mystic type."[71] Many of the other themes that the two novels share are probably a result of a common social milieu. For example, the fear of insanity would not be an uncommon fear for women around 1910 when so much was being written about hysteria[72] and when woman's supposed psychological insufficiencies was often a reason given for denying women the vote. In addition to a common social milieu, both writers had their roots in a common literary tradition — that of the Brontës, *Villette* especially, as well as Wells's novels of ideas and of social criticism.

CHAPTER 7

Life and Death of Harriett Frean

THE protagonists of most stream-of-consciousness novels, such as those of Joyce, Richardson, and Virginia Woolf, are characters like Mary Olivier in that, because they are endowed with a high degree of perceptiveness and sensitivity, they provide their creators with rich and interesting material. May Sinclair in her next psychological novel, *Life and Death of Harriett Frean* (1920), took as her protagonist a woman almost the opposite of this type in that she has a particularly unimaginative and restricted consciousness. To Sinclair's credit, she managed, despite her unpromising heroine, to write a novel that is compelling, even exciting, and one that also demonstrates that the stream-of-consciousness technique can be successfully applied to a wide range of character types.

I A "Good" Woman

Harriett Frean portrays the inner life of a woman who has been so thoroughly taught by her parents to practice self-sacrifice and self-denial that she becomes emotionally impoverished and totally lacking in individuality. Unlike Mary Olivier, Harriett Frean has neither the intelligence nor the strength of character to rebel against her parents' values and to seek her own values. As a result of these inabilities, she becomes a mere shadow of her parents, is enveloped in a cocoon of middle-class cant, and is driven to some pathetic self-deceptions to protect herself from the realization that her values are questionable or that her life has been empty and wasted. Being more than just a portrayal of an individual, the novel is a criticism of a whole social class and of the parents' ideal of family life, since their trying to adhere to the ideal of the "holy family" suffocates and sterilizes the child.

Harriett Frean's parents are enlightened and sophisticated people in mid-nineteenth-century England, for her father reads Darwin and

Herbert Spencer and writes articles for the *Spectator*. They lead a genteel life, believe in isolating their daughter from everything they consider ugly, and try to rear her according to the ideal of "behaving beautifully." They are too enlightened to forbid her anything explicitly; instead, she must behave as they wish because they trust her and because she would make them unhappy if she did not. At a children's tea party, Harriett has one of her first experiences of the pains and greater rewards of self-denial when the hostess by mistake gives her piece of cake to another child. Harriett's mother affectionately praises her, "I'm glad my little girl didn't snatch and push. It's better to go without than to take from other people. That's ugly."[1] One of her few attempts at independence in her childhood is effectively squelched when she one day walks alone through the disreputable part of the town against which she has been warned. Her father tells her she must not go there again because doing so makes her mother unhappy: "Forget ugly things. Understand Hatty, nothing is forbidden. We don't forbid, because we trust you to do what we wish. To behave beautifully."[2]

With this kind of inner control from her parents — a control more insidious than Mrs. Olivier's arbitrary pronouncements — Harriett becomes the prisoner of her parents' ideals. When Robin, the fiancé of her friend Prissy, falls in love with her, she sends him back to her friend because it is the honorable and beautiful thing to do. Because of the pain of her loss, she turns to her parents for comfort; and her adult young life is centered around her family: they read together; take annual trips to the continent together; and, in general, form a self-sufficient unit. Harriett loses the habit of consulting her own feelings and follows their wishes in matters important and trivial. For example, when her mother consults her about whether she would prefer to move to Sidmouth or to Hampstead, Harriett, even though she would prefer to live in Sidmouth, chooses Hampstead because she thinks her mother would prefer it.

At times, Harriett realizes that her ideal of self-sacrifice can be destructive both to herself and to others, but she has neither the imagination nor the courage to be deeply bothered by this realization or to change. For example, during her visit to Prissy and Robin a few years after their marriage, Harriett discovers that her decision to send Robin back to Prissy has benefited nobody. Since her marriage, Prissy suffers from an undiagnosed illness that has paralyzed her and made her an invalid-wife who requires Robin's constant care and attention. In spite of the pitiful state to which Prissy has been reduced, Harriett is jealous of her; but she never questions the rightness of her decision or of the ideal of "behaving beautifully" that had inspired it. Not being very perceptive or given to self-analysis, Harriett masks her jealousy of Prissy with what she considers to be a generous and unselfish feeling of pity for her. By the third night of her visit, Robin's unhappiness and resentment of his marriage become unmistakably clear even to Harriett; but she turns away from this realization because it threatens the ideals by which she lives.

After her mother's death, Harriett begins to feel vulnerable, insecure, and almost lost. She feels that part of herself has died because she had so completely merged her own life with her mother's, and she finds it difficult to maintain the illusion of being "intellectual," superior to others, and self-sufficient. Never having read for her own delight but only to please her parents and to join in their activity, she is bored by their favorite authors now that she is alone. When the feeling of emptiness comes to her, she begins visiting her childhood friends, where she sits for hours talking and passing away her time: "She found that by a system of punctual movements she could give her existence the reasonable appearance of an aim."[3]

After a year's mourning, Harriett makes some pathetic attempts at self-expression. She changes vicars: "She left her mother's Dr. Braithwaite, who was broad and twice married, and went to Canon Wrench, who was unmarried and high. There was something stimulating in the short, happy service, the rich music, the incense and the processions." She makes new covers for the drawing room; she turns from her parents' serious reading material to light novels; and, finally, "as she had always had the cutlets broiled plain because her mother liked them that way, now she had them breaded." The futility of this bit of habitual self-denial from Harriett's past is underlined by the maid's comment, "That was how the mistress always had them, ma'am, when you was away."[4] Despite Harriett's self-assertion, she has little confidence in herself; indeed, her favorite means of asserting her own worth and her own importance becomes "My father was Hilton Frean."[5]

Her attempts to screen herself from any recognition of the emptiness and the futility of her life lead her to some minor and major cruelties. She fences her yard to keep out a neighboring cat, which she finds offensive because of its quick movements, its liveliness. When her unmarried maid is going to have a baby, she offers to let her return after the baby's birth because that would be "the beautiful thing to do." But, once the baby is in the house, she cannot bear the sight of it: "She decided that Maggie must go. Maggie was not doing her work properly. Harriett found flue under the bed."[6]

As Harriett shrinks into the life of the aged, the poor, and the lonely, her only pleasures become eating, sleeping, and being among familiar objects and childhood friends. Gradually, she begins to feel safe and comfortable only in her own home where she is looked after by her maid, on whom she becomes completely dependent, almost as if her maid were her mother and she a little girl again. When she falls ill at age seventy, she is proud that she has the same illness that her mother had had. When she consents to an operation, her greatest fear is that she will say indecent things under the influence of the anesthetic; but the nurses comfort her by telling her that, if she keeps her mouth shut tightly before the operation, she will be all right. On the morning of the operation, she refuses to speak, communicates by gestures, and walks to the operating room with a look of exaltation on her face. When she gets there, "Harriett made her tight lips tighter. She climbed on to the white enamel table, and lay down, drawing her dressing gown straight about her knees. She had not said one word. She had behaved beautifully."[7]

Under the influence of the anesthetic, Harriett's defenses fall and many of the feelings she has habitually suppressed in her mind are expressed — her fears about sex, her guilt feelings for having sent Maggie's baby away, her desire to have been Prissy and have had a baby, her desire to be a little girl again and be comforted by her mother:

She knew that the little man they called the doctor was really Mr. Hancock. They oughtn't to have let him in. She cried out. "Take him away. Don't let him touch me;" but nobody took any notice. "It isn't right," she said.

"He oughtn't to do it. Not to any woman. If it was known he would be punished."

And there was Maggie by the curtain crying.

"That's Maggie. She's crying because she thinks I killed her baby."

The ice bag laid across her body stirred like a live thing as the ice melted, then it settled and was still. She put her hand down and felt the smooth, cold oilskin. . . .

"It's sad — sad to go through so much pain and then to have a dead baby."

The white curtain walls of the cubicle contracted, closed in on her. She was lying at the bottom of her white-curtained nursery cot. She felt weak and diminished, small like a very little child. . . . She smiled with a sudden ecstatic wonder and recognition. "Mamma —"[8]

This novel can be regarded as having been inspired by the new psychology inasmuch as it depicts the evils of repression. Harriett's habit of denying her feelings leads to sterility, suffering, and some cruelties necessary to evade her realization of her own situation. Only in the last scene do her defenses come down and her repressed feelings surface. The psychological ideas are completely assimilated to a full realization of Harriett's character; and they have a textbook flavor only in a scene in which a young woman, who is defending herself for marrying her friend's fiancé, gives Harriett what amounts to a lecture about the evils of self-sacrifice.

II *Criticism of Victorian Values*

Being more than just a study of repression, the novel provides implicitly a criticism of conventional ideals of self-denial, of moral rectitude, of an ideal of family life, and possibly of a whole social class whose refinement ultimately leads to sterility. Not surprisingly, *Harriett Frean* caught the eye of Lytton Strachey, who read it and recommended it to Virginia Woolf.[9] Sinclair's intent was not to mock eminent Victorians for their self-importance and priggishness, as Strachey does, but to show the seeds of sterility and waste in refined gentility. In this respect, the novel is closer to the spirit of E. M. Forster and D. H. Lawrence than to Strachey. Like Sinclair's other psychological novels, it implicitly favors cultivating one's individuality and joining the spirit to the flesh.

Although the social implications of the novel are not directly stated, they are implied and reinforced by the imagery. Repeated throughout the novel is the image of a workbox, a hollow blue egg that opens along its circumference to store scissors, thimble, and thread. This egglike workbox, a wedding present to Harriett's parents, is on display in the living room where it intrigues Harriett as a child. After her mother's death, when Harriett is asserting her individuality by redecorating the living room, she puts the workbox away. In her old age, when she feels comforted by the presence of familiar things, she displays it again.

This egglike workbox, the only recurring image in the novel, stands for fertility and sex that are domesticated into the Victorian ideal of family life and, like the workbox, made hollow. The scissors and thimble it contains and the fact that the child Harriett keeps calling it an egg emphasize its sexual implications. The fact that the workbox was a wedding present to Harriett's parents and the description of its being decorated on the top with a "gold ball with a frill round it like a crown" suggest the ideal of family life to which the Victorians paid homage and which the Freans cultivate. In middle age, Harriett puts the workbox away, in an attempt to break away from the confines of her family and to express, however feebly, her own individuality. In her old age, when she can only buoy up her self-confidence with the words, "My father was Hilton Frean," it goes on display again. At the end of the novel, when she is being operated on for a tumor, she thinks she has just delivered a dead baby. The egglike workbox represents an ideal of family life whose only issue is waste — a tumor, a dead baby.

In contrast to the workbox are the red campion flowers, suggestive of passion and sex, that grow in the disreputable part of the neighborhood where her parents have forbidden her to go. Harriett, in a spirit of adventure and defiance, saunters there one day and admires the flowers, only to be rescued by her frightened mother. The interlocking symbols of campion flowers, workbox, and dead baby are used to imply a criticism of the Victorian ideal of domesticity and family life that represses instincts and leads to sterility.

III   Use of Stream of Consciousness

May Sinclair referred to this novel as an experiment[10] in compressing a long life in the shortest possible narrative and in the welding of the stream of consciousness to more traditional techniques. The ruthless economy she practiced and her use at times of traditional methods of narration helped Sinclair to overcome the rambling and pointless quality that seems to afflict such stream-of-consciousness novels as *Pilgrimage* and to create a novel that is aesthetically unified. Her use at times of traditional omniscient methods of narration helped her overcome the second shortcoming of the stream-of-consciousness novel — the tendency of the author and the protagonist to be fused so that no aesthetic distance exists between the two. Virginia Woolf, writing before Joyce's *Ulysses*, was referring to this problem when she wrote, "The danger is the damned egotistical self, which ruins Joyce and Richardson to my mind; is one pliant and rich enough to provide a wall for the book from oneself. . . .[11]

One of the results of this identification between author and protagonist in the earliest stream-of-consciousness novels is that the author has no way of indicating the difference between the way things really are and the way they appear to his protagonist. For example, critics have frequently indicated that Miriam Henderson in the first chapters of *Pilgrimage* and Stephen Dedalus in *Portrait of the Artist as a Young Man* seem to be actually but unawarely egocentric and priggish and that the authors seem to accept their protagonists' own evaluation of themselves. Sinclair noted this problem in the stream-of-consciousness technique: "This method has its limitations — you are confined to one consciousness, you share its prejudices and its blindnesses, you know no more of the other people in the book than it knows, but you get a much more vivid and real presentation of that particular character's life than you would by standing outside it. . . . All the time the author naturally does know more than his character, and he must present things so that they appear both as they really are and as they appear to the consciousness of his one subject."[12]

In *Harriett Frean* Sinclair faced and overcame this problem by being at times the omniscient author. For example, when Harriett learns that Prissy is paralyzed, she muses at length over the pity she feels for Prissy; and then the narrator adds: "She saw the paralysis as coming between them, separating them, and inside her the secret pain was soothed. She need not think of Robin married any more."[13] At times Sinclair conveyed the difference by first presenting Harriett Frean's stream of consciousness and then the verbal conclusion that Harriett draws, which is usually a conclusion that denies or rationalizes everything in her thoughts that is damaging to her self-esteem. For example, when some neighbors who write for the *Spectator* do not return her second call, Harriett feels rebuffed and lonely: "She was old, old. She had nothing in common with middle age, with intellectual exclusive people connected with the *Spectator*. She said, 'The *Spectator* is not what it used to be in my father's time.'"[14]

Although other writers also tackled the problem of using the stream-of-consciousness technique in such a way that the author could communicate a perspective wider than that exhibited by the consciousness of his characters, as Joyce did in *Ulysses*, with great brilliance and inventiveness, Sinclair in *Harriett Frean* was one of the first to tackle this problem. In using the stream-of-consciousness technique in conjunction with traditional methods of narration, May Sinclair also pointed the way to the future effective use of this technique. For example, Virginia Woolf in *Mrs. Dalloway* and in *To the Lighthouse* used stream of consciousness with conventional methods of narration; and the stream of consciousness entered the main course of fiction in this combination rather than in the purer form used by Joyce and Richardson. Although Dorothy Richardson presented Miriam's actions and thoughts from the focal point of an omniscient author, the omniscience is confined to Miriam's thoughts; and, since the author identifies herself completely with Miriam, no other perspective is found in the novel but Miriam's.[15]

Critics have argued that tying oneself exclusively to the stream-of-consciousness technique can be stultifying and that this method of narration is most effectively used as Sinclair used it — in combination with traditional methods. In a recent article, a critic has written,"Our compulsion to have all fact and action in the novel 'mediated' through character has lumbered us with a set of conventions that seem to have utterly exhausted their utility and expressiveness. So far from aiding the process and effect of representation, these conventions now seem to come clumsily between ourselves and what is represented. . . . the novel cannot survive without what James calls 'authorship' "[16] — that is, the author's acting as narrator and commentator.

Sinclair used the stream of consciousness to gain greater vividness, immediacy, and fullness in depicting character; but she comments and narrates to achieve unity and a level of reality outside her subject's consciousness against which the subject can be judged. Sinclair looked upon the stream of consciousness not as a means of communicating feminine sensibility as Richardson did, nor as a means for gaining artistic autonomy and impersonality as Joyce did, nor as a means of recapturing the past as Proust did; she regarded it more simply as a means of gaining greater immediacy and vividness in depicting a character. Hence she would not consider conventional methods of narration inherently wrong or inartistic if, by using them at times, she could gain unity and a broader perspective than she could have by adhering throughout the novel to an apparently unselected stream of consciousness.

IV *Evaluation*

In 1921, the new psychology was considered by the vast majority of the public to be in itself disreputable if not sinister. In a series of articles on the new psychology featured in the *Pall Mall Gazette*, one of the expositors of the new psychology writing about Freud referred to "the obscene bent of his mind" while another wrote about the "unwholesomeness of morbid introspection."[17] Many of the reviewers of *Harriett Frean* reflected this dislike or at least suspicion of the new psychology, for many of them seemed to find fault with the novel just because it was psychological.

The review in the *Times Literary Supplement* was titled "A Mother Complex" and began thus: "Miss May Sinclair's mind seems to be still brooding over what is commonly called the new psychology." The reviewer had some words of praise for the novel, but concluded that it "is a study in pathology, rather than a story of the generic truth of human nature."[18] T. S. Eliot also qualified his praise by noting that the novel shows the influence of some psychoanalytic ideas and hence "rests upon a dubious and contentious branch of science."[19] J. D. Beresford in a French journal in 1926 summed up the state of public opinion about psychoanalysis when he wrote that "all novelists who wish to be received well by the public and by the press cannot ignore those restrictions placed on them about treating questions of psychoanalysis. . . . and the novelist who wants to treat this subject ought to know to what fatal hostility he is going to expose himself."[20]

Only the reviewers of the more liberal periodicals, the *Nation* and the *New Republic*, did not criticize Sinclair's novel for making use of some ideas from psychoanalysis. Indeed, the reviewer in the *New Republic* justly noted that the psychology is completely assimilated and that, rather than being about a mother complex, shows the "crippling and binding power of living by acquired catchword standards."[21]

In terms of technique, *Harriett Frean* is in certain ways an advance over her other novels. As opposed to *Mary Olivier*, the writing in this novel is economical, precise, and tight; for Sinclair relates in one hundred and thirty-three pages a life of seventy years. Yet the impressionistic style makes it rich in suggestion; for, phrases, statements, and images, which are presented without any comment by the author, produce for the reader flashes of illumination about the meagerness of Harriett's life and about her pathetic self-deceptions. The plot is tightly organized and moves swiftly from the climax, when Harriett rejects Robin, to the reversal, when Harriett is living alone, and to the resolution in the final scene on the operating table, a scene that is the climactic epiphany of her repressions and her sterility. In part, the tightness of the structure and the economy make the effect of the novel so powerful. T. S. Eliot, for example, referred to the pity and terror the novel evokes.[22]

Yet *Harriett Frean* lacks not only the scope of *Mary Olivier* and of

The Three Sisters but also some of their vitality. Being a novella, it is limited to the single objective of showing the makings and the workings of a repressed woman. Despite the fact that *Mary Olivier* and *The Three Sisters* are also concerned with the plight of the single woman in Victorian society, they are much richer novels, because *The Three Sisters* captures the quality of different kinds of sexual passion, and *Mary Olivier* is a coming-of-age novel that depicts the development and changes in Mary Olivier, as well as the effects of the family on Mary's three brothers and on her two aunts. In contrast to Mary Olivier, Harriett is at the beginning what she is at the end, and no subsidiary characters enlarge and deepen the novel. Gwenda and Mary are characters who elude any formula or any final definition, whereas Harriett retains no mystery and no opacity. She is too clearly and only a repressed woman. Indeed, Sinclair seemed to have exhausted her material about the plight of the single woman in this novel, for she never again worked directly or exclusively with this subject. In fact, a few months after she had finished *Harriett Frean,* she showed almost a distaste for the subject in her reply to a request that she write an article on unmarried women: "I'm not interested in the Superfluous 2,000,000! If they *are* superfluous, let them emigrate. But they don't and won't."[23]

In certain respects Sinclair's treatment of the problem of the single woman in *Harriett Frean* is more unsparing and severe than in her previous novels. The culprits are not individual ogres like the crotchety vicar or the domineering Mrs. Olivier, but kind and well meaning people like Harriett's parents. In addition, Harriett does not become a finer person as a result of her self-sacrifice (as Gwenda does) nor does she find God (as Mary does). In fact, Sinclair seemed to be taking pleasure in puncturing the concept of self-sacrifice that was so important to her idealistic philosophy; for Harriett's giving up Robin is destructive both for Harriett and for the other people involved; and the ideal of self-sacrifice is viewed as the mechanism whereby Harriett is crushed both as a woman and as a human being.

Sinclair's changing attitude toward the ideal of self-sacrifice may have been a reaction to her belief, frequently expressed in the war years, that young men who lost their lives in the war had by their self-sacrifice ennobled themselves and had been brought closer to God. After the war, she seemed to have felt a repugnance to this glorifying of war by glorifying the ideal of self-sacrifice. Something of this change in her attitude comes out in two letters she wrote to Hugh Walpole. In 1916, she praised *The Dark Forest,* in which the protagonist's death at the front is presented as a victory for him, as a "magnificent book" and the "best war book of this war." In the same letter she described Henry James's funeral and wrote, "How proud he would be about *The Dark Forest*. He loved our soldiers and he has gone over with a glorious company."[24] But three years later in a letter in which she criticized Walpole's latest novel, *The Secret City*, she impatiently dismissed *The Dark Forest*. "Why," she wrote, "did you . . . follow up the older and by now irrelevant trail of *The Dark Forest*."[25] As is evident also from some of her subsequent novels, by 1919 Sinclair's attitude toward the war had changed. Some of the vengeful spirit with which she deflated the ideal of self-sacrifice in *Harriett Frean* may have been a reaction against the part this ideal had played in glorifying a war that no longer seemed so glorious.

V *Psychoanalytic Problem Novels*

After *Harriett Frean*, Sinclair was never again concerned chiefly with the problem of the superfluous woman or with a novel that was psychological either in using the stream-of-consciousness method or in attempting to capture by other means the subjective inner life of her characters. Although she wrote two problem novels — *The Romantic* and *Anne Severn and the Fieldings* — that illustrated certain psychoanalytic concepts, they are not very successful or memorable; they were attempts to convince the public of the value of psychoanalytic ideas in helping to free people from wasteful and destructive lives.

The Romantic (1920) is told from the point of view of Charlotte Redhead, who falls in love with a young man and goes with him to the front as part of an ambulance unit. Recovering from a previous love affair, Charlotte is happy with John even though he avoids any physical consummation of their love. While on the field collecting the wounded under fire, John is at first ecstatic and then frightened and cruel to Charlotte. Because he exposes Charlotte to danger while he hides, Charlotte realizes that he is a coward and that he hates her because she has seen his cowardice. After John is killed on the field, a doctor explains to Charlotte that John had romanticized danger and had regarded war as a happy adventure because he was impotent. The thrills of danger and his success at times in overcoming his fear had become a substitute for sexual satisfaction and power. He was cruel to Charlotte whenever he was cowardly because, not having gained a sense of power by withstanding danger, he experienced it by dominating people. Since the point of view is Charlotte's but the narrative is about John, John is seen entirely from the outside; and, as a result, he has no greater reality than a character in a case history. The social message of this slight, two hundred and three page novel seems to be that cruelty and romanticizing of war can be a manifestation of psychological disturbance and sexual frustration.

The same criticism applies to *Anne Severn and the Fieldings* (1922); for, as in *The Romantic,* a doctor is introduced to reveal the motivations of the characters and to drive home the message which is, in this case, that repressing one's fears is destructive and that happiness and freedom can only be reached by facing them. The story is about the love affair of Anne with one of the Fielding brothers, Jerrold, a young man who cannot face human suffering. After Anne nurses his father through a fatal illness, Jerrold jilts her because she has become associated in his mind with the scenes of his father's suffering. To escape his memories, he marries a young woman he does not love. The human propensity to attempt to escape unpleasantness is repeated in the fate of Jerrold's brother, Colin, who returns from the war a victim of shell shock, discovers that both his mother and his wife want nothing to do with him, and finds that only Anne will care for him until he recovers. Jerrold's wife, Maisie, realizing that her husband does not love her, develops a psychosomatic illness; leads the life of an invalid; but, when a doctor reveals to her the cause of her illness, she recovers and gives Jerrold a divorce so that he can marry Anne. In this triangle of a man and two women and one frequently present in Sinclair's novels, self-sacrifice is, for the first time, not the answer. Instead, psychoanalysis sheds the light that leads to the enlightenment and happiness of all concerned.

The novel is narrated by a more or less omniscient narrator, and Anne's consciousness is treated more fully than that of the others. Jerrold and Maisie, about whose emotional subterfuges the plot turns, are developed in such a cursory fashion that the reader is told about their emotional vagaries rather than made to feel them. Anne also is not a fully realized character. She is Sinclair's ideal "new woman" — capable nurse, efficient manager of a large farm, emotionally generous and daring in taking Colin to live with her so that she can take care of him, and finally passionate lover of Jerrold. Anne's story represents Sinclair's wish fulfillment: Anne is adopted by a family that has only sons; two of them fall in love with her; she finally marries Jerrold, who like Sinclair's favorite brother (Mark in *Mary Olivier*) has served in India. Anne and Jerrold are kept apart for a time by Jerrold's mother, who tells him lies about Anne. After Sinclair completed this novel, she was not very enthusiastic about it, writing that she liked it least of all the novels she had done in the last few years.[26]

Life and Death of Harriett Frean, The Romantic, and *Anne Severn and the Fieldings* all imply the need to bring together physical and spiritual qualities to achieve wholeness as a human being. One of Sinclair's objections to Christianity was its dualism — the division between body and soul, spirit and flesh — which she believed "is the root of half the evil and the sickness and the suffering in the modern world."[27] Sinclair wrote these lines during the first world war to explain why eastern mysticism, in which both body and soul are accepted, is preferable to Christianity.

Although Sinclair believed that body and spirit should be brought together, most of her female characters, such as Gwenda and Mary Olivier, never succeed in doing so, as if a woman could not have a sexual relationship in marriage and at the same time maintain her integrity of mind and personality.[28] But to conclude because of this that Sinclair believed that self-sacrifice is a woman's destiny by nature would not represent her mature viewpoint in *Harriett Frean* in which self-sacrifice is clearly a value imposed by Harriett's parents. In *Anne Severn and the Fieldings,* Anne successfully combines both masculine and feminine virtues. She is a resourceful, active, sensitive, tender and passionate woman who marries her lover, and yet Anne has none of the authenticity and reality of Sinclair's portraits of thwarted women; she is merely the illustration of an idea. Sinclair never drew a convincing portrait of a sexually fulfilled androgynous heroine, perhaps because few such women existed in her world.

CHAPTER 8

Final Novels

A FTER *Harriett Frean,* Sinclair's best work was not her
two psychological problem novels but her two comic novels that
unmask two members of the English ruling class, an egotistical country squire in *Mr. Waddington of Wyck* (1921) and a lazy rector in *A
Cure of Souls* (1923). These two novels show a new spirit of tolerance
toward human follies and weaknesses, but they also imply a serious
criticism of the middle class by unmasking both its temporal and
spiritual leaders and by suggesting their hollowness. Sinclair's
amused but critical detachment that appears in these novels lasted
only a few years; for by 1924 she retreated to the assurances of her
idealistic philosophy and started writing novels that were largely
poor imitations of her earlier works.

I Mr. Waddington of Wyck

Mr. Waddington of Wyck is about the wealthy squire Horatio
Bysshe Waddington, whose family has owned Wyck Manor for ten
generations, thereby giving him the ascendency over Sir John
Corbett, a wealthier and larger landowner whose family has been in
Wyck for only fifty years. Mr. Waddington is a colossal egoist, and
with advancing age — he has just turned fifty — his need to assert
his ego seems to be increasing. When the story begins, he is working
on a book about the Cotswold countryside, one which he thinks will
bring him the recognition his gifts merit but one which is actually
atrociously bad. His secretary's annoying habit of suggesting
changes in the manuscript prompts Waddington to fire him and to
replace him with a new secretary, a more docile young woman. The
novel dramatizes three episodes, all of which are essentially Mr.
Waddington's fruitless attempts to express his ego: he tries to start in
Wyck a branch of the National League of Liberty, an anti-

Bolshevist, antisocialist reactionary organization; he tries to seduce an attractive widow in the village; and he finally proposes marriage to his new secretary. In each of these escapades, he makes such a fool of himself that he emerges as a comic figure who is more a victim of his own folly than a victimizer of others.

Early in the narrative, Waddington has accepted the invitation of the London office of the National League of Liberty to start a branch in Wyck; and he anticipates becoming its president. But, after a few meetings during which he takes great pleasure in making long pompous speeches, the villagers are so bored they gradually lose interest and stop attending. Mr. Waddington blames the failure of the League on the fact that Wyck is a sleepy place and that its citizens are not interested in wider issues.

When an attractive war widow in Wyck suggests that he evict one of his farm laborers and remodel the cottage into a suitable house for her, he conceives the idea of making her his mistress. A shrewd woman, she succeeds by lies and flattery in getting Mr. Waddington to let her have the cottage rent free and then applies to him for a "loan" of five hundred pounds. In an interview in which she realizes that Mr. Waddington is not going to give her the money unless she becomes his mistress, she teases him until he starts making love to her and then she gets her revenge by feigning outrage and heaping abuse upon him in the presence of his secretary. Although Mr. Waddington comes to believe his own story that the widow was trying to seduce him, he has unguarded moments when he recalls the truth about his attempted seduction; in these moments he soothes his ego by attributing his attempt to his ungovernable youthful passion and his failure to her unnatural coldness.

After Mr. Waddington's secretary, Barbara, has helped rescue him from the widow, who had threatened him with blackmail, he assumes that Barbara must be in love with him and he decides to marry her. In anticipation of this event, he buys some splashy clothes — a yellow vest and two pairs of pajamas covered with a pattern of forked lightning. When he proposes marriage to Barbara, she protests that she does not love him and that she is engaged to his former secretary, Bevan. Mr. Waddington, who cannot conceive of her preferring another man, rationalizes that she loves him but is marrying Bevan because she does not want to hurt his wife by destroying their marriage. To Barbara's surprise, his reply to her rejection of him is, "Poor child, so that is what I have driven you to."[1]

Aghast at his inference, blinded by the yellowness of the new vest he
is wearing, and thinking of the forked pajamas she had caught a
glimpse of, Barbara is overcome by laughter. Her laughter punctures
his self-esteem only momentarily; for, as Barbara is leaving the
room, he is muttering to himself, "That child is a saint, a saint."[2]

In addition to providing glimpses into Mr. Waddington's mind,
Sinclair shows him from the point of view of at least seven other
characters in the novel. Much of the comedy is in the contrast in
different scenes between Mr. Waddington's view of himself and that
of these other characters who are aware of his folly. Yet each
character regards him differently and does so according to the
breadth of his own nature and sympathies: the widow works on his
vanity to get money out of him; Sir John, a large landowner, is aware
of his folly but respects him for his position; Mr. Waddington's son,
himself an egoist but cleverer than his father, regards him as an em-
barrassment and as a dullard about whom he can make fun in order
to display his own cleverness; to his young secretary, Barbara, his
vanity is a source of boundless amusement. Of his lies she says,
"moral indignation would have been a false note; it would have
been downright irreverance toward the God that made him."[3]
Through most of the novel, Mr. Waddington is seen from the point
of view of Barbara, and the reader shares her delight in him.

Only in the closing pages of the novel is Mr. Waddington seen
from the point of view of his wife, and the reader becomes aware of
the pathos and waste of his life. His wife, sorry that Barbara has rejected her husband, remarks about his proposal, "I was glad. I
thought if only he could have one real feeling."[4] She considers
herself responsible for much of the emptiness in his life because she
had married him without loving him. In the last page of the novel,
Mr. Waddington is on his way to see his eighty-year-old mother. His
wife knows that his mother, who dotes on him and who still treats
him like a young man, will soothe his vanity. Sinclair's interweaving
of the different perspectives from which Waddington is viewed is
masterfully done; and, although Barbara's point of view
predominates and produces a comic novel, the last pages add a tragic
dimension.

In certain respects, *Mr. Waddington of Wyck* is a feminist novel
that exposes the follies of the male climacteric and suggests that the
traditional feminine role the women in his life play is responsible for
much of the falsity in Mr. Waddington's life. Although he is past the
age of needing to be mothered, his mother still clings to her role; his

wife marries him without loving him because of the social pressure upon her to catch a husband; and both his secretary and his wife, playing the traditional feminine role, finally do their best to protect his ego by pretending to believe his lies and by shielding him from a knowledge of the truth. In contrast to the women, Waddington's male secretary does not think his role is to devote himself to protecting Mr. Waddington's ego. To dwell on the feminist aspect of the novel would be, however, to distort its emphasis, which is upon the comic scenes in which Mr. Waddington tries to seduce the widow and in which he proposes marriage to Barbara. Solemn, pompous, and fat, Mr. Waddington sees himself as an irresistible lover. He is unaware of the effect he is having, and when the women start to repulse him, he pursues them more ardently. We see him mostly through Barbara's eyes as a modern Malvolio. The feminist aspects discussed are merely suggested in the few lines that describe his mother's attitude toward him and his wife's reasons for marrying him. Other than these lines there is no overt social or psychological commentary in the novel.

Sinclair manages to retain the reader's sympathy for Mr. Waddington in spite of his part in starting a National League of Liberty and in evicting a farm laborer from his cottage. Ralph Bevan, Barbara's fiancé, regards the League as a sinister organization — as an attempt to discredit the rise of laborers by instilling fear of Bolshevism and socialism. But Bevan also recognizes that Mr. Waddington is a tool of the leaders of the group in London; that Mr. Waddington's interest in politics is minimal; and that the organization is merely a way of his feeding his ego. Very little ill will exists in Waddington, and the socialists in the village who shout him down at the village hall are among the anxious inquirers after his health when he gets influenza. Sinclair also diverts the reader's condemnation of Waddington for evicting his farm laborer because he does so after the ambitious widow lies to him when she relates that the laborer has been calling him abusive names. By providing extenuating circumstances for Waddington's two sinister actions, the novel remains an essentially genial one. Yet it has serious social and political implications, for Mr. Waddington in these two actions is presented as a member of the ruling class and as one who is unfitted for his task.

This work is one of Sinclair's most finely and delicately balanced novels, for the moral issues are not always clear cut, the comedy and the pathos coexist, and Mr. Waddington remains a sympathetic figure in spite of the fact that in his actions, if not in his motives, he is at times both a villain and a fool. If one considers the serious implications of the novel, Mr. Waddington emerges, like Harriett Frean, as a figure of waste and sterility. Though he has a son, he takes little pleasure in him; in fact, he regards him as a threat and as a reminder of his advancing age. His wife says that Waddington was happiest during the war when he held a civilian post in the village. Like Harriett at the end of the novel, he is ready to fall into his mother's arms. In certain respects Waddington, like Harriett, is a victim of the social system and of the frustration of his sexual instincts that is underscored by the pattern of forked lightning on his pajamas. Although Sinclair does not explicitly make the connection, much of his futile and sometimes harmful behavior stems from his attempts to compensate for his frustations.

II   A Cure of Souls

A *Cure of Souls* can be viewed as a companion novel to *Mr. Waddington of Wyck,* for its protagonist, the Reverend Canon Clement Purcell Chamberlain, is as much as Horatio Bysshe Waddington an example of the sterility and incapacity of the English ruling class; and, like *Mr. Waddington,* it is a delightfully comic narrative with serious overtones. Canon Chamberlain, a bachelor at forty-three, is an easy, lazy, epicurean clergyman whose usual state of lassitude, both physical and moral, is threatened by his curates. His junior curate is a strenuous Christian who believes in bringing Christ to the working classes through youth clubs and other programs; his senior curate Jackman is going through a spiritual crisis and is beginning to doubt the existence of God; and much of the humor derives from the clash between the rector's values and those of his curates. In one scene, Jackman, the senior curate, goes to the rector's home to seek spiritual help and advice; he finds the rector having his tea; he shyly withholds telling the rector the purpose of his visit; and then, "Choosing the moment when the Rector had got his teeth into the first hot, rich slice of buttered crumpet, he let himself go."[5] While Jackman talks around the subject, the rector offers him the comforts of tea and crumpets:

> The young man drank a little tea obediently and then stopped as if it had choked him. He rose and stood up awkwardly, holding his cup and saucer at a dangerous angle.
> The Rector thought: In another minute he'll spill his tea and ruin my best Bokhara rug. And he'll smash that cup, too.

Bokhara rugs and Spode china didn't exist for Mr. Jackman in his mood. He didn't care what became of them. The Rector rose and took his cup from him and insisted on his sitting down.

"Now then," he said, "we can talk comfortably." He helped himself to another bit of buttered crumpet. He had filled the slop-bowl with boiling water and set the crumpets on the top to keep them hot. "What do you say the trouble is?"[6]

After Jackman finally confesses that he can no longer believe in God, the rector stops eating crumpet: "This was terrible. Jackman could not have started a topic more subversive of all peace. He almost hated Jackman."[7] During the conversation that follows about the meaning of suffering, the horrors of the last war, and the nature of God, the rector's thoughts keep straying to the crumpets. At one point, the rector, seeing that none of his theological arguments are convincing Jackman, offers the opinion that the source of Jackman's trouble is not really religious doubt but poor health; and he suggests that Jackman eat fresh fruit every morning. " 'You think,' said Mr. Jackman, with a sudden dreadful humour, 'I should find God if I ate fresh fruit?' "[8] As the interview continues, Jackman gives way to despair; the rector maintains a steady stream of comforting religious platitudes; but, inwardly, his despair over the ruined crumpets almost matches Jackman's over the loss of God.

Aside from having to placate his curates, the only other difficulty in the rector's life is overcoming the nonconformists' opposition to having the war memorial built in his church instead of in the village square where they wish it to be. By the end of the novel, the rector is restored to his placid state: he marries a rich plump widow who enjoys good food and a peaceful lazy life as much as he does; he wins his way with the war memorial; his strenuous curate is transferred to another parish; and his doubting curate, Jackman, leaves the clergy to become a social worker.

The rector is clearly identified with the English upper class and with what Sinclair considered to be its limitations. He dislikes having to pray for the well being of the present government — Lloyd George's coalition — when he would like to pray for the return to power of the Tories. His one political interest is that Germany be made to pay war reparations. Although he is the essence of laziness and sloth, he believes, as he says in one sermon, that "the general unrest and trouble of our time is due to enforced idleness, to the existence in our midst of an immense body of unemployed."[9] Much of his failure when his parishioners turn to him for help is caused by his incapacity for strong emotion and by his discomfort in the presence of any expression of strong emotion because "He always felt that there was something indecent about it."[10] His most devoted parishioners are the old ladies, whose favorite topic of conversation is their illnesses, and the few sex-starved young women who do all his parish visiting for him.

The novel is rich in irony, for the rector is singularly unsuited to "a cure of souls." The novel opens with a long scene of the rector's waking up and enjoying his warm bed, his morning toilette, and his breakfast. Before his breakfast, he says a perfunctory prayer during which he feels "a light tension of constraint, his attitude before the Immaterial." Although he finds praying not as pleasurable as his other morning activities it, "like the discharge of any regular function, . . . gave relief."[11] The only duty he performs with real pleasure and care is having his excellent cook make rich soup for any ailing parishioners. But, when he is called upon to help them spiritually he fails, partly out of laziness and partly out of his feeling of helplessness and irritability in the presence of strong emotions.

In one scene, the rector is called out of his bed to administer the last sacrament to a poor dying woman who lives in a remote part of his parish. When he arrives at her home, he is so repelled by the stale odors of the poor cottage and by the crying of her grieving daughter that he can hardly bring himself to approach the deathbed; and, as a result, the parishioner who rode him there has to comfort the dying woman and her family. When the rector hears the next morning that the woman had failed to die during the night, he feels more than ever that his parishioners are inconsiderate and unfair. Sinclair manages to keep the tone of even this episode comic; the humor resides in the basic irony of the situation of a minister who cannot and does not like "to minister" and in the discomfiture of the comfort-loving rector as he is dragged out of his pleasant sleep and then goes on his long ride in an open cart through the drenching rain.

The only sinister note is sounded when the rector encourages a hysterical religious spinster to fall in love with him so that he can have her to do all his parish visiting for him. When he marries, the spinster has a nervous breakdown; and her doctor, who had warned him against encouraging her, is shocked by his callousness. The rector's encouragement of her infatuation has been, however, almost unconscious, since his acting to ensure his peace and his comfort has become so habitual for him that he is incapable of making any other choice. Indeed, the reader sees the rector enjoying his slothful ease so thoroughly while he is eating a bowl of strawberries or resting in his garden that he hardly seems a sinister figure

At the time of Sinclair's death in 1946, the writer of her obituary in the *Times* selected *A Cure of Souls* for special praise and described it as "complete, rounded and humourous" and as "May Sinclair at her best."[12] At the time, however, of the publication of this novel, the reviewers tended to find somewhat distressing the implied social criticism in the novel and her ironical portrayal of a Church of England priest. The reviewer in the conservative *Spectator* acknowledged that the novel was "delightful to read, charming and amusing," but he found fault with the characterization of the rector because "he has no virtues to balance his sins."[13] The *New York Times,* in one of its rare comments about books in the editorial page, posed the question: "What have the clergy of Great Britain's Established Church been doing to antagonize and offend English authors?" The writer thought Sinclair's book cruel "for her 'villain' gets no punishment, but achieves the 'happy ending' which ought to be the reward of virtue alone."[14] In the liberal *Nation,* the reviewer was just as distressed that Sinclair should take such a good-humored view of an essentially tragic situation and criticized her for being too detached, for seeming to be "perched above the tumult."[15]

III   *Short Stories*

In the years 1922 and 1923, Sinclair also wrote a number of short stories of fantasy in which she has a similar detached and humorous view about human follies and weaknesses. Unlike her earlier ghost stories, which were mostly psychological and psychical and in which the tone was often ominous, these later stories of fantasy are ethical and metaphysical parables based on various ideas of idealistic philosophy; and the tone is often a humorous one. For example, "The Victim" develops the idea of the unreality of evil when it is gauged by a metaphysically absolute point of view. A ghost returns to thank his tormented murderer for delivering him out of a tight spot — he was about to be declared bankrupt. "Jones's Karma," a parable about fate and free will, shows through Jones that character determines one's choices and that these become one's fate.

In "The Finding of the Absolute," a philosopher, his wife, and her

poet-lover find themselves in heaven together. The respectable husband is shocked and puzzled, for he thinks the adulterous couple
should be housed elsewhere. But he learns, before he is absorbed
into the absolute and loses his sense of separateness and identity,
that the intensity of his wife's love for the poet, the lover's dedication to poetry, and his own passion for truth are all godly attributes
that have brought them all to heaven. In "Heaven," Sinclair
returned once again to the theme of the domineering mother. A
young man dies and to his surprise finds himself in a heaven that
seems to be tailored to his mother's beliefs — religious services,
punctilious and circumspect behavior, priggish and pompous angels,
and banal conversations. At first, he is bored; then he finds it dis-
tasteful; and, finally, repulsive. At this point, he is transferred to
another heaven which is not described very much but which, the
reader is given to understand, is more to his liking and more fitting
to his higher state of moral consciousness. He is told that his mother
had willed him into her own heaven, but his own strong feelings
make him able to will himself out of it.

In these short stories, as in Sinclair's two comic novels, the tone is
gentle, often humorous; and evil is seen as a lower level of moral
consciousness. The rector has not developed beyond the sensuous
level; the squire, beyond the level of personal vanity; and the
mother in "Heaven," beyond middle-class respectability. "Heaven"
shows none of the passion that had gone into the depiction of the
conflict between parents and children in Sinclair's psychological
novels; instead, these short stories, as well as her comic novels, show
a new spirit of detachment — one which in "Jones's Karma" is ex-
tolled as the "path of perfect freedom." The guru, who tells the
parable of Jones, concludes by saying that free will and determinism
are pairs of opposites and that, so long as one affirms the reality of
opposites, he is subject to illusions. Man is free of these illusions
"when it is indifferent to a man whether he is himself or not himself,
whether he lives or dies, whether he catches the cholera or does not
catch the cholera. Thus he escapes from desiring and undesiring,
from the pairs of opposites, and from the chain of happenings and
the round of births."[16] To a certain extent this Indian philosophy is
compatible with philosophical idealism, according to which opposites are reconciled and transcended in the absolute.

Two of these stories appeared in the *Criterion*. In fact, the first
page of "The Victim" faced the last page of T. S. Eliot's "The Waste
Land." To Herbert Howarth, who has argued that these stories in-

fluenced T. S. Eliot,[17] certain lines in "Dry Salvages" and in "Little Gidding" echo lines and ideas from "Jones's Karma" as well as from Sinclair's *Defence of Idealism.* T. S. Eliot was probably impressed by some of these works because they dealt with metaphysical ideas with which he was himself struggling at the time. In themselves and in comparison to some of her other novels, these stories are not very vital or memorable; and Sinclair herself spoke slightingly of them. "I am amusing myself by writing ghost stories," she wrote in 1921.[18] To T. S. Eliot, who apparently had some good things to say about "The Finding of the Absolute," she wrote, "I'm glad you did not think the Absolute [*sic*] so absolutely worthless as I was afraid it was."[19] These short stories mark the reassertion of her metaphysical interests, for she also published in 1922 her second book on philosophy, *The New Idealism.*

IV   Arnold Waterlow *and Later Novels*

In *Arnold Waterlow* (1924), *The Dark Night* (1924), and *The Rector of Wyck* (1925), the novels that followed *A Cure of Souls,* Sinclair was again writing sympathetically about acts of self-sacrifice, which, as in *Mary Olivier,* were shown to lead to a mystical experience of the presence of God; moreover, these three novels conclude with the protagonist's finding God after experiences of great suffering. In *The Dark Night,* the protagonist goes through the stations of the mystic way, including the dark night of the soul; in *The Rector of Wyck,* almost as if she were compensating for her portrait of the rector in *A Cure of Souls,* Sinclair created a rector who is a true man of God, Christlike in his compassion and suffering. Whereas idealistic mystical ideas in *Mary Olivier* are presented as a possible resting point for a fully realized quest, these later novels seem to have been written from a set of convictions; and the experiences through which these concepts are expressed are shadowy and unconvincing.

The novels she wrote after *A Cure of Souls* are increasingly poor because she was evidently casting about for material and was reworking her previous novels. In *Arnold Waterlow,* she repeats many of the situations in *Mary Olivier* and is essentially redoing that novel with a male protagonist; in *Waterlow,* she included material from a poem and a character sketch that had appeared years ago in *The Egoist.*[20] The tensions that had generated her best novels, the conflict between mother and child and the problems of the dependent woman, are no longer strongly felt situations in these final novels. In fact, in *The Rector of Wyck* the rector's daughter, who refuses to return to Wyck to look after her aging father is drawn as a cold, hard-hearted woman.

These novels and even more so the three that followed them — *Far End* (1926), *The Allinghams* (1927), and *History of Anthony Waring* (1927) — tend to be sentimental and melodramatic. With *The Rector of Wyck*, Sinclair apparently lost her interest in experimental or modern techniques; and this novel, as well as her subsequent ones, are all conventionally written and the chief interest lies in the narrative. By 1925, it is evident from her novels that her failing health had also affected her creative and critical powers.

E. M. Forster, who was sixteen years younger than May Sinclair, stopped writing novels after 1924 because he felt that the world had changed so radically. By 1924, Sinclair was sixty-one years old; and her world had changed considerably from the Victorian world in which she had reached middle age. But Sinclair continued to write because she needed money and had to earn a living. She had always been generous in helping friends and relatives in need and in spending for causes in which she believed. In 1915, she wrote to a friend that she was on the "bedrock" of her "natural income,"[21]; and she not only apologized in 1917 about the small check she was sending in response to a request for contributions but explained that until her next novel was published, she was at her "means' end."[22] Sinclair's need for money explains the rapid rate at which she published during her final years; after *A Cure of Souls* she published six novels between 1924 and 1927, the date of her last novel. The fact that her last six novels were so poor was probably one of the reasons she was so thoroughly forgotten. At the same time, unfortunately, her other novels, some of them of permanent value, shared the fate of the inferior ones.

CHAPTER 9

Conclusion

B Y reading May Sinclair's novels, one gains a better perspective
on the genesis of the modern novel. The influence of Henry
James, Thomas Hardy, and the Brontës on the modern novel, frequently referred to but difficult to trace in the works of Sinclair's
more famous contemporaries, is apparent in Sinclair's novels. In addition, the importance of philosophical idealism in Sinclair's novels
suggests a certain continuity between the Victorian and the modern
intellectual beliefs that contributed to the making of the psychological novel. Mrs. Humphry Ward may have been the spokes-
man for this philosophy, but one also finds traces of it in the novels
of Henry James and Dorothy Richardson. Through Sinclair's works,
one also sees a close relationship between imagism and the modern
novel — a relationship that, except for certain statements made by
Ezra Pound, Ford Madox Ford, and Dorothy Richardson, is not
otherwise easily documented. Finally, through Sinclair's novels one
gains a more just assessment of the novels of D. H. Lawrence and
Dorothy Richardson. D. H. Lawrence in some of his characteristic
themes was one voice among others; Dorothy Richardson in
Pilgrimage is not *sui generis* or a follower of G. E. Moore, but she
shares with Sinclair a commitment to mysticism and to philosophical
idealism. Beginning with an attempt to place Sinclair in relationship
to her contemporaries, one ends by knowing her contemporaries
better.

Paul West in his book, *The Modern Novel*, concluded his evaluation of May Sinclair's achievement by regretting the influence of
psychoanalysis on her works; and he thereby echoes the same
criticism most frequently leveled against her writings by her contemporaries. To West, "Unfortunately May Sinclair never got over the
novelty of the new psychological science; unfortunately, because she

had the intelligence to write a masterpiece about even the feminist cause."[1] This criticism does not seem to be warranted when one compares her psychological novels to the novels which preceded them. Her psychological novels are so markedly superior to her other novels, with the exception of A Cure of Souls, that one must conclude that psychoanalysis had a liberating and enriching effect upon her work.

That she never wrote a masterpiece is less attributable to her not recovering from the novelty of psychoanalysis than it is, perhaps, to the very intelligence that Paul West cites: she was a fiercely intelligent and intellectual woman. Almost completely self-educated and lacking any of the advantages of growing up in an intellectual atmosphere, she taught herself Greek, enough Sanscrit to read the Indian classics, and both French and German. She also mastered all the important works in philosophy and then did her own creative work in this area. A series of letters to Bertrand Russell indicates that she had also tried to go through his books on mathematical logic, although not without some difficulty.[2]

This type of scholarly, systematic and metaphysical cast of mind is not, perhaps, the most promising for literary creativity. Because she lacked what Keats referred to as "negative capability," she was continually fitting the experiences she wrote about into formulated and abstract schemata of one sort or another: first, into the theories of philosophical idealism; second, to theories of naturalism; third, to those of psychoanalysis; and, fourth, to her former schema of philosophical idealism. She was aware of this shortcoming herself when she referred to her "special vice, a love for too much neatness and completeness of idea."[3]

Although May Sinclair in her reviews of other writers' works was often enthusiastic, wholehearted, and confident, she showed a certain diffidence about her own work. While this timidity about her own capabilities enabled her to learn from the criticisms of others, it also had the unfortunate effect of making her rely too much upon other writers for models: H. G. Wells for The Combined Maze, the Brontës for The Three Sisters, and Richardson for Mary Olivier. She did not have the self-confident ego of men like Lawrence, Joyce, and Yeats who, whatever their sources, created works that were unmistakably their own. Sinclair was reared in a home and lived in an age in which women who did not fit the mold were subject to a great deal of emotional bullying that was bound to leave its mark.

Sinclair was also a child of her era in her moral and ethical earnestness. Her art suffers when, as in *The Romantic* and in *Anne Severn and the Fieldings* as well as in sections of *The Three Sisters* and *Harriett Frean*, she tried to reform her readers' values by advancing certain psychoanalytic ideas. She was a social reformer; and, although she cautioned Wells against being too preoccupied with ideas in his novels, she herself succumbed to this tendency.

Yet May Sinclair made some contributions to the English novel and to English literature. She was one of the first English novelists to absorb the theories of psychoanalysis and to make creative use of them in *The Three Sisters*, and this novel adumbrates the lifelong themes of D. H. Lawrence. By her awareness and expression of her characters' unconscious — the sexual drives of the Cartaret sisters, the dreams of Mary Olivier, and the final unconscious musings of Harriett Frean — Sinclair brought into her novels a level of reality deeper than that which existed in the realistic novels of the previous decade.

Sinclair has also been considered one of the pioneers in the stream-of-consciousness novel; for, according to Dawson Scott, Sinclair was experimenting with this technique "before Dorothy Richardson began to write."[4] Most likely this critic had in mind some of Sinclair's Jamesian short stories and early novels, in which she used the interior monologue and a central intelligence instead of an omniscient narrator; for Sinclair was indebted to Richardson's *Pilgrimage* for the stream of consciousness she used in *Mary Olivier.*

Sinclair's originality in connection with the stream-of-consciousness novel was in her critical appreciation of its aims and methods, which she revealed in her critical article about *Pilgrimage.* In this article, she gave adequate definition, sympathetic understanding, and enthusiastic support to the stream-of-consciousness novel which most critics at that time misunderstood and which, as a result, they regarded unsympathetically and critically. All later criticism of the stream-of-consciousness novel, including Virginia Woolf's essay "Modern Fiction," is strongly indebted to Sinclair's article. In Sinclair's own use of the stream of consciousness in *Mary Olivier* and *Harriett Frean*, she made a number of modifications which made the style more readable and also assimilated it to other more traditional methods of structuring novels.

Not the least of Sinclair's contributions to the English novel was in helping to bury Mrs. Grundy's standards in literature by writing about sex in greater detail and with more honesty than critics of her time desired or approved. Sinclair was also a discriminating critic of modern poetry and played a part in fostering some of the best poets of her day, most of whom at the time were still unrecognized.

If one looks for the continuation of the tradition of Sinclair's novels among present day novelists, the writers who come to mind are Doris Lessing, Ivy Compton-Burnett, and L. P. Hartley. In her series of novels on Martha Quest and in her *Golden Notebook* Lessing seems to be continuing the tradition of Richardson's *Pilgrimage* and Sinclair's *Mary Olivier* by writing about women who are trying to break out of the confines of their family, to overcome the blind spots of their society, and to come to terms with their lives by trying out different philosophies and points of view. Compton-Burnett drew the materials for her novels from the Victorian family structure of her girlhood, and many of her sinister family situations with domineering mothers and ambivalent children are very similar to the family situations in Sinclair's novels.

L. P. Hartley, who as a young man wrote reviews of two of Sinclair's later novels,[5] develops in his Eustace and Hilda series and especially in his *The Shrimp and the Anemone*, which he started writing in the 1920s, many of Sinclair's characteristic themes. His protagonist, Eustace, feels the rival claims of self-denial and self-expression; there is a suggestion of an incestuous love for his sister; and, like one of Sinclair's protagonists, he stands aloof from passionate life and finds his greatest happiness in luminous moments of a mystical nature.

Finally, many of Sinclair's works can be read with pleasure for their own sake. Through the corpus of her work from *Superseded* in 1902 to *A Cure of Souls* in 1924 she presented a comprehensive view of English society of the time and provided the reader with the pleasure of seeing an intelligent, courageous, and honest mind dealing with the problems and recreating the ambience of the time. She was a distinguished and careful stylist who wrote with wit, grace, and subtlety. In her novels, Sinclair showed an imaginative sympathy for and an ability to create a wide range of characters from many classes and social milieus, from the lower middle-class Rannie Ransom in *The Combined Maze*, the farmer Jim Greatorex and the servant Essy and her mother in *The Three Sisters*, to the squire and rector in her comic novels. Between these two classes, and most often, she wrote about English middle-class family life: the effete gentility of the London Freans; the harsh puritanism of the Vicar

Cartaret in a Yorkshire village; and the sacrifice of individual thought, feeling, and aspiration to the tyranny of good manners and conformity of the suburban Ilford Oliviers.

She was at her best in recreating the world of the middle-class, dependent women in late Victorian times. Beginning with Juliana Quincey in *Superseded* and going on to the vicar's daughters in *Three Sisters*, the three maiden aunts in *Tree of Heaven,* Mary Olivier and her two maiden aunts, and Harriett Frean, Sinclair recreated the social and psychological life of these women with a completeness, sensitivity, and honesty that one seldom finds in her contemporaries. Forty years ago Horace Gregory wrote that "May Sinclair is still alive today in a sense that both H. G. Wells and Arnold Bennett can never be again." Referring to Wells's *Ann Veronica* and Bennett's *Clayhanger,* he asserted that their heroines are no longer exciting and that the reader tends to look upon them "with amusement."[6] Much of the continued viability of Sinclair's novels stems from her recreation of the lives of these women. Sinclair will survive as a novelist with her own particular vision because of her portraits of the dependent and often repressed women of her era in *Superseded, The Three Sisters, Mary Olivier,* and *Life and Death of Harriett Frean.*

Today, all but two of Sinclair's novels are, unfortunately, out of print; and, as a result, her work has not been properly assessed. Many critics tend to dismiss Sinclair as a mere popularizer of modern trends, perhaps because they are repeating the critical response to her later inferior work or to the popularly successful *The Divine Fire.* Some of her admirers, trying to redress the balance in her critical reputation have overstated her achievements. In 1972, perhaps in response to the new interest in women writers, *Mary Olivier* was reissued, and a few provocative articles on that novel have followed. Clearly, the first step in the assessment of her work would be the reissue of her best novels. For their intrinsic merit and for the light they shed on the history of the modern novel, May Sinclair's two other psychological novels *(The Three Sisters* and *Life and Death of Harriett Frean), Superseded,* and *A Cure of Souls* should be made available again.

Notes and References

Preface

1. William Lyon Phelps, *The Advance of the English Novel* (New York, 1916), p. 226. See also Abel Chevalley, *The Modern English Novel* (London, 1925), p. 200.

2. Frank Swinnerton, *The Georgian Scene: A Literary Panorama* (New York, 1934), p. 381.

3. Joseph Warren Beach, *English Literature of the Nineteenth and Early Twentieth Centuries* (New York, 1962), p. 244.

4. Walter Allen, "Introduction," in *Pilgrimage* by Dorothy Richardson (London, 1967), I, 3 - 4.

Chapter One

1. For the dates of May Sinclair's birth, of her mother's death, and of her attendance at Cheltenham Ladies College see T. E. M. Boll, "May Sinclair: A Checklist," *Bulletin of the New York Public Library* 74 (September, 1970), 454.

2. *A Journal of Impressions in Belgium* (London, 1915), p. 28.

3. Theophilus E. M. Boll, *Miss May Sinclair: Novelist* (Rutherford, N.J., 1973), p. 25.

4. Willis Steell, "May Sinclair Tells Why She Isn't a Poet," *The Literary Digest International Book Review* 2 (June, 1924), 513.

5. Boll, *Miss May Sinclair*, p. 244.

6. Ibid., pp. 27 - 28.

7. I. A. R. Wylie, *My Life with George: an Unconventional Autobiography* (New York, 1940), p. 178.

8. R. Walker, "May Sinclair Talks of Everything Except Herself," *New York Times Book Review*, May 18, 1924, p. 2.

9. Rebecca West, unpublished letter to author, December 4, 1968.

10. May Sinclair to Edward Garnett, June 15, 1911, University of Texas Library.

11. Samuel Hynes, *The Edwardian Turn of Mind* (Princeton, 1968), p. 276.

12. Harry T. Moore, *The Intelligent Heart: the Story of D. H. Lawrence* (London, 1954), p. 260.

13. There are many references to the help Sinclair gave others in the memoirs of her contemporaries. See, for example, Curtis Brown, *Contacts* (New York, 1935), p. 49.

14. Elizabeth Raikes, *Dorothea Beale of Cheltenham* (London, 1908), pp. 389 - 90.

15. Ibid., p. 392.

16. Ibid., p. 393.

17. Ibid., p. 394.

18. May Sinclair, "The Ethical and Religious Import of Idealism," *The New World* 2 (December, 1893), 694 - 708.

19. Bertrand Russell, "Philosophical Idealism at Bay," *Nation and Athenaeum* 31 (August 5, 1922), 625.

20. R. G. Collingwood, letter to publisher, August 21, 1922, Macmillan Collection, New York Public Library.

21. Anon., *Proceedings of the Aristotelian Society*, n.s. 23 (1923), 281.

22. "Primary and Secondary Consciousness," *Proceedings of the Aristotelian Society*, n.s. 23 (1923), 111 - 20.

23. Melvin Richter, *The Politics of Conscience: T. H. Green and His Age* (Cambridge, Mass., 1964), pp. 183 - 85. See also "T. H. Green," in *Encyclopedia of Religion and Ethics*, ed. James Hastings (Edinburgh and New York, 1908 - 1926), VI, 439.

24. "The Import of Idealism," p. 703.

25. Anne Fremantle, *This Little Band of Prophets: The British Fabians* (New York, 1960), p. 157.

26. Warren Wagar, *H. G. Wells and the World State* (New Haven, 1961), p. 107.

27. Richard Ellmann, "The Two Faces of Edward," in *Edwardians and Late Victorians*, English Institute Essays, 1959, ed. Richard Ellmann (New York, 1960), pp. 198 - 200.

28. "The Import of Idealism," p. 702.

29. Dorothea Krook, *Ordeal of Consciousness* (Cambridge, England, 1962), pp. 410 - 11.

30. Dorothy Richardson, "Deadlock," in *Pilgrimage* (London, 1967), III, 23, 41, 162, 171, 175.

31. Richardson, "The Tunnel," in *Pilgrimage*, II, 236 - 37.

32. "The Import of Idealism," p. 703.

33. Richter, p. 14.

34. "Josiah Royce," *Biographical Dictionary of Parapsychology* (New York, 1964), p. 275.

35. Lawrence Jones, "Note," *Journal of the Society for Psychical Research* 17 (February, 1915), 25.

36. Lawrence Jones, *An Edwardian Youth* (London, 1956), pp. 9ff.

37. J. A. Hobson, *L. T. Hobhouse* (London, 1931), p. 184.

38. "Symbolism and Sublimation II," *Medical Press and Circular* 153 (August 16, 1916), 142.

39. "People in the Foreground: Miss May Sinclair," *Current Literature* 38, no. 3 (March, 1905), 223.

40. Anon., "May Sinclair Circular," Publicity Material, Macmillan Collection, New York Public Library.

41. May Sinclair to Theodore Roosevelt, May 11, 1912, Library of Congress. Sinclair did not accept the invitation.

42. May Sinclair to Otto Kyllmann, November 24, 1905, Northwestern University Library. In a later letter to Mr. Kyllmann, she wrote, "The Americans are still bent on giving me 'the time of my life' " (December 12, 1905). She enjoyed meeting Orne Jewett and William James, whom she thought "delightful"; but her hosts, Henry Holt and his daughter, were apparently overzealous in arranging engagements for her and in keeping her entertained. On Christmas day, she escaped and toured the Negro section of Boston (Sinclair to Otto Kyllmann, December 25, 1905, Northwestern University Library).

43. Ernest Rhys, *Everyman Remembers* (New York, 1931), p. 302.

44. Elizabeth Jordan, *Three Rousing Cheers* (New York, 1938), p 183.

45. May Sinclair to Mrs. Myer, September 10, 1906, Yale University Library.

46. May Sinclair to Edward Garnett, January 15, 1905, University of Texas Library.

47. May Sinclair to Otto Kyllmann, October 18, 1908, Northwestern University Library.

48. William Lyon Phelps, *Autobiography with Letters* (London, 1939), pp. 551 - 52.

49. May Sinclair to Annie Fields, July 16, 1912, Henry E. Huntington Library.

50. Ford Madox Ford, *Return to Yesterday, Reminiscences 1894 - 1914* (London, 1931), p. 371.

51. "Three American Poets of Today: Edward Arlington Robinson, William Vaughan Moody and Ridgely Torrence," *Atlantic Monthly* 98 (September, 1906), 326.

52. May Sinclair to Charlotte Mary Mew, July 17, 1913, Berg Collection, New York Public Library.

53. "The Reputation of Ezra Pound," *English Review* 30 (April, 1920), 327.

54. Ibid., p. 329.

55. May Sinclair to Charlotte Mary Mew, July 17, 1913, Berg Collection, New York Public Library.

56. Robert Frost, *Selected Letters*, ed. Lawrence Thompson (New York, 1964), p. 74.

57. Ibid., p. 70.

58. May Sinclair also tried to help Eliot financially when he was ill in 1923. Sinclair, together with Richard Aldington and Ezra Pound, was a lifetime member of the "Bel Esprit" society. The purpose of this society was to provide a lifetime income for Eliot by having thirty members contribute ten pounds yearly toward his support. See Ezra Pound, *Letters 1907 - 1914*, ed. D. D. Paige (New York, 1950), p. 175.

59. " 'Prufrock and Other Observations,' A Criticism," *The Little Review* 4 (December, 1917), 12.

60. John Wain, "Poetry," in *The Twentieth-Century Mind: History, Ideas, and Literature in Britain*, ed. C. B. Cox and A. E. Dyson (London, 1972), I, 407.

61. Sinclair, " 'Prufrock,' " pp. 12 - 13.

62. Ibid., pp. 10 - 11.

63. Ibid., p. 12.

64. A. R. Jones, "Notes Towards a History of Imagism," *South Atlantic Quarterly* 60 (Summer, 1961), 264. Pound made a similar claim about Ford, then known as Hueffer, in "Mr. Hueffer and the Prose Tradition in Verse," in *Pavannes and Divisions* (New York, 1918), p. 137.

65. Ford Madox Ford, ed., "Foreward: Those Were the Days," in *Imagist Anthology* (New York, 1930), p. 18.

66. Reinald Hoops, *Der Einfluss der Psychoanalyse auf die Englische Literatur* (Heidelberg, 1934), p. 41.

67. "Symbolism and Sublimation I," *Medical Press and Circular* 153 (August 9, 1916), 120.

68. May Sinclair to T. S. Eliot, March 17, 1922, Harvard University Library.

69. Before moving into her house in 1914, Sinclair had lived in a flat, and for ten years (1897 - 1907) in rented rooms (Sinclair to Sarah Orne Jewett, August 29, 1907, Harvard University Library).

70. Rebecca West, unpublished letter to author, December 4, 1968.

71. Wyndham Lewis, *Letters*, ed. W. K. Rose (London, 1963), p. 139. Wyndham Lewis sent Sinclair a gift of two drawings of faces for which she thanked him in an undated letter in the Cornell University Library.

72. Douglas Goldring, *South Lodge* (London, 1943), p. 115.

73. Ella Hepworth Dixon, *As I Knew Them: Sketches of People I Met on the Way* (London, 1930), p. 125.

74. Boll, "May Sinclair: A Checklist," p. 458.

Chapter Two

1. At the time of its publication, *The Divine Fire* was said to have been suggested by Ernest Dowson's career. Like Dowson, Rickman is a gifted poet who leads a disorderly life, but also works hard as a translator and has the same fierce pride that keeps him from appealing to anyone for help. See

John Gasworth, "The Dowson Legend," *Transactions of the Royal Society of Literature*, n.s. 17 (1938), 106.

2. "The Import of Idealism," p. 702.

3. Ibid., p. 703.

4. Ibid., p. 705.

5. Ford Madox Ford, "Literary Portrait VI, Miss May Sinclair," *The Tribune*, August 31, 1907, p. 2.

6. C. C. Vernam to anonymous editor, June 1, 1906, Macmillan Collection, New York Public Library.

7. "The Cosmopolitan," in *The Return of the Prodigal* (New York, 1914), p. 355.

8. Ibid., p. 362.

9. May Sinclair to Charlotte Mary Mew, April 22, 1915, Berg Collection, New York Public Library.

10. F. W. Dupee, *Henry James* (New York, 1956), p. 56.

11. May Sinclair to Edward Garnett, March 12, 1902?, University of Texas Library.

12. W. C. Frierson, *The English Novel in Transition* (Norman, Okla., 1942), p. 112.

13. "The Cosmopolitan."

14. Ibid., p. 358.

15. May Sinclair to Edward Garnett, March 12, 1902?, University of Texas Library.

16. May Sinclair to Edward Garnett, January 15, 1905, University of Texas Library.

17. May Sinclair to Edward Garnett, March 20, 1902, University of Texas Library, quoting from his letter to her.

18. May Sinclair to Edward Garnett, May 17, 1908, University of Texas Library.

19. Ford Madox Ford, "Literary Portrait VI, Miss May Sinclair," p. 2. Ford gave a slightly different version of the same story in *Return to Yesterday: Reminiscences 1894 - 1914* (London, 1931), p. 326.

20. Copy of May Sinclair's will, probated February 1947, Principal Probate Registry, Somerset House. The portrait may have been a photograph of the Sargent painting. James sent a signed photograph of the painting to the three hundred admirers who had commissioned the portrait in honor of his seventieth birthday. See Leon Edel, *Henry James, The Master: 1901 - 1916* (New York, 1972), p. 486.

21. This gift may also have been Sinclair's homage to the memory of Robert Singleton Garnett's father, Richard Garnett, who had been very kind to Sinclair when she first arrived in London. She had also been helped by the criticism of Richard's other son, Edward Garnett.

22. Phelps, *Autobiography with Letters*, p. 552.

23. May Sinclair to Hugh Walpole, April 12, 1912, University of Texas Library.

24. May Sinclair to Hugh Walpole, March 5, 1918, University of Texas Library.

Chapter Three

1. Upton Sinclair, *My Lifetime in Letters* (Columbia, Mo., 1960), p. 299.
2. T. E. M. Boll in "*The Divine Fire* (1904) and *Martin Eden* (1909)" points to a number of similarities between the two novels, and argues that Jack London was influenced by Sinclair's novel. See *English Literature in Transition, 1880 - 1920* 14, no. 2 (1971), 115 - 17.
3. *Audrey Craven* (New York, 1906), p. 11.
4. Anon., "Literary Personalities: The Author of the Divine Fire," *The Outlook* 81 (November 25, 1905), 728.
5. *Two Sides of a Question* (London, 1901), p. 240.
6. Ibid., p. 291.
7. Ibid., p. 222.
8. Ibid., p. 307.
9. Ibid., p. 223.
10. Frierson, p. 129.
11. Lawrence Jones, *An Edwardian Youth*, pp. 162 - 63.
12. Walter E. Houghton, *The Victorian Frame of Mind, 1830 - 1870* (New Haven, 1957), p. 351.
13. *The Helpmate* (New York, 1907), p. 47.
14. Ibid., pp. 425 - 26.
15. Ibid., p. 423.
16. May Sinclair to Bertrand Russell, November 14, 1917, Bertrand Russell Archives, Mills Memorial Library, McMaster University.
17. Violet Hunt, *I Have This to Say: The Story of my Flurried Years* (New York, 1926), p. 51.
18. "George Meredith," *Outlook* 92 (June 19, 1909), 416.
19. *Feminism* (The Women Writers Suffrage League, 1912), p. 20.
20. Anon., "The Helpmate," *Times Literary Supplement*, September 6, 1907, p. 269a.
21. Ford Madox Ford, "Literary Portraits VI," p. 2.
22. *The Judgment of Eve* (New York, 1908), p. 105.
23. Ibid., pp. 121 - 22.
24. Ibid., p. 8.
25. "Man and Superman: A Symposium," *New York Times Literary Section*, December 1, 1905, pp. 813 - 14. The published article was an "unrevised proof" and not the revised version (Sinclair to Otto Kyllmann, December 12, 1905, Northwestern University Library).
26. *The Immortal Moment: The Story of Kitty Tailleur* (New York, 1908), p. 306.
27. Lady Robert Cecil, "The Cant of Unconventionality," *The Living Age* 38 (December 7, 1907), 585; reprinted from the *National Review*.

28. Ibid., p. 583.

29. May Sinclair to Thomas Hardy, October 31, 1910, Dorset County Museum, Thomas Hardy Collection.

30. Ford Madox Ford thought that the portrait of Tanquery was modeled on himself. He obviously was not pleased, for he referred to Tanquery as "a villain" and surmised that Sinclair was still angry with him about his comments about *The Divine Fire*. Actually, Tanquery is sympathetically drawn, except for his callous treatment of the women in his life; but he is also shown to be irresistibly attractive to all the women in the novel and the most gifted novelist in the circle on whom all the others rely for critical advice and judgment. Ford, *Return to Yesterday*, p. 371.

31. May Sinclair to Richard W. Gilder, March 10, 1909, University of Texas Library.

32. May Sinclair to Annie Fields, January 9, 1909, Henry E. Huntington Library.

33. May Sinclair to Annie Fields, August 3, 1910, Henry E. Huntington Library.

34. May Sinclair to Ford Madox Ford, October 28, 1910, Berg Collection, New York Public Library.

35. *The Combined Maze* (New York, 1913), p. 87.

36. Ibid., p. 343.

37. Ibid., p. 320.

38. Ibid., p. 366.

39. Anon., "The Combined Maze," *Times Literary Supplement*, February 20, 1913, p. 76b.

40. Vincent Brome, *H. G. Wells* (London, 1951), p. 112.

41. *The Helpmate*, p. 426.

42. May Sinclair to H. G. Wells, June 29, 1919, University of Illinois Library, Urbana.

43. May Sinclair to Edward Garnett, June 15, 1911, University of Texas Library.

44. May Sinclair to H. G. Wells, October 16, 1915, University of Illinois Library, Urbana.

45. H. G. Wells, *The Passionate Friends*, 2nd ed. (London, 1914), pp. 194 - 95.

46. H. G. Wells, *The New Machiavelli* (London, n.d.), pp. 295 - 96.

Chapter Four

1. Arthur Waugh, *Tradition and Change* (London, 1919), p. 206.

2. Ibid., p. 214.

3. Havelock Ellis, "Auto-Eroticism," in *Studies in the Psychology of Sex* (New York, 1936), I, 219.

4. Frederick J. Hoffman, *Freudianism and the Literary Mind* (Baton Rouge, 1957), p. 44.

5. Hoops, p. 41.

6. Theophilus E. M. Boll, "May Sinclair and the Medico-Psychological Clinic of London," *Proceedings of the American Philosophical Society* 106 (August, 1962), 312.

7. Ibid., pp. 313, 316.

8. "Symbolism and Sublimation I," p. 120.

9. "Symbolism and Sublimation II," p. 144.

10. Ibid.

11. *A Defence of Idealism* (New York, 1917), p. 9.

12. Carl G. Jung, *Psychology of the Unconscious* (New York, 1916), p. 479.

13. "Symbolism and Sublimation II," p. 142.

14. *A Defence of Idealism*, p. 7.

15. "Psychological Types," *English Review* 36 (May, 1923), 438.

16. *A Defence of Idealism*, p. 267, 287, 289, 293, 338, 339.

17. *Audrey Craven* (New York, 1906), p. 266.

18. The character of Audrey Craven, as well as some of the plot, seems to be a reworking of George Moore's "Mildred Lawson," one of the short stories in *Celibates* (1895). Moore modeled Mildred Lawson on the writer Mrs. Craigie, whose pen name was John Oliver Hobbes. She had collaborated with Moore on plays and had been a good friend of his until she rejected him as a lover. Moore took his revenge by drawing this satirical portrait of her as an unfeeling flirt. See Vineta Colby, *The Singular Anomaly: Women Novelists of the Nineteenth Century* (New York and London, 1970), pp. 210 - 19.

By introducing into her version of Moore's story an author who writes a novel about Audrey Craven, Sinclair included in her novel the circumstances of the authorship of "Mildred Lawson." Not only does the respected critic in the novel, Knowles, lecture Wyndham on the limitations of realism, but he also ends his friendship with Wyndham for dishonorably taking advantage of a woman's trust to collect material for a novel.

19. *The Judgment of Eve and Other Stories* (London, 1914), p. xii.

20. "The Gift," *Fortnightly Review* 90 (September, 1908), 533.

21. "Between the Lines," in *Tales Told by Simpson* (New York, 1930), p. 106.

22. Ibid., p. 113.

23. Ibid., p. 114.

24. Sinclair to Thomas Hardy, July 21, 1909, Dorset County Museum, Thomas Hardy Collection.

25. *The Three Brontës* (New York, 1912), p. 139.

26. "Introduction," in *Villette* by Charlotte Brontë (London, 1909), p. x.

27. "Introduction," in *Jane Eyre* by Charlotte Brontë (London, 1908), p. viii.

28. *The Three Brontës*, p. 139.

29. "Introduction," *Jane Eyre*, p. xvi.

30. Ibid., p. viii.

31. "Introduction," in *The Tenant of Wildfell Hall* by Anne Brontë (London, 1914), p. xii.

32. *The Three Brontës*, pp. 149 - 50.

33. "Introduction," *Villette*, pp. xiv - xv.

34. Dorothy Richardson found the same inspiration in *Villette*. Miriam Henderson in *Pilgrimage* states that she first read *Villette* when she was fifteen and since that time whenever she finishes it, she begins it again.

35. *The Three Brontës*, p. 123.

36. Ibid., p. 146.

37. *The Three Sisters* (New York, 1914), pp. 378 - 79.

38. Ibid., pp. 184 - 85.

39. Ibid., p. 370.

40. Ibid.

41. Ibid., p. 179.

42. Pierre Janet, *The Mental State of Hystericals* (New York, 1901), p. 526.

43. Gregory Zilboorg and George Henry, *A History of Medical Psychology* (New York, 1941), p. 376.

44. Ellis, p. 233.

45. Ibid., p. 232.

46. Ibid., p. 234.

47. Ibid., p. 218.

48. *The Three Sisters*, p. 77.

49. Sir Almroth Wright, "On Suffrage Fallacies," *The Times*, March 28, 1912, p. 8.

50. Ibid. Shaw's portrait of Colenso Ridgeon in *The Doctor's Dilemma* is based on Sir Almroth Wright. Shaw indirectly poked fun at Sir Almroth's views about women by showing Ridgeon acting as emotionally and as irrationally as the heroine. See Louis Compton, *Shaw the Dramatist: A Study of the Intellectual Background of the Major Plays* (London, 1971), pp. 124, 139 - 40.

51. Cecil Woodham-Smith, *Florence Nightingale 1820 - 1910* (London, 1950), pp. 93 - 94.

52. Ibid., p. 437.

53. Jones, *An Edwardian Youth*, p. 138.

54. W. L. Burn, *The Age of Equipoise: A Study of the Mid-Victorian Generation* (New York, 1964), p. 249.

55. Anon., "The Three Sisters," *The Nation* 94 (November, 1914), 632.

56. *The Three Sisters*, p. 40.

57. Ibid.

58. The image of the moon appears often in Charlotte Brontë's novels, as Robert B. Heilman has noted in "Charlotte Bronte, Reason, and the Moon,"

Nineteenth Century Fiction 14 (March, 1960), 283 - 302. He concludes, however, that "we cannot finally assign an explicit symbolic value to Charlotte's moon."

59. Lawrence's "Two Marriages" was published posthumously in *Time and Tide* 15 (March 24, 1934), 393 - 99. Although Lawrence had written "Daughters of the Vicar" by 1913, he kept revising the story even while working on the page proofs in October 1914. D. H. Lawrence, *Letters*, ed. Aldous Huxley (New York, 1932), p. 213, 218.

60. D. H. Lawrence, "Daughters of the Vicar," in *The Prussian Officer and Other Stories* (London, 1929), p. 118.

61. *The Three Sisters*, p. 121.

62. Lawrence, "Daughters of the Vicar," p. 125.

63. Lawrence, "Two Marriages," p. 393.

64. Lawrence, "Daughters of the Vicar," p. 65.

65. Ibid.

66. Lawrence said about Sinclair, "Why do you like May Sinclair so much over here [in America]? You should see her, a little humped up scrawny woman. Oh, married, of course, but she could never be anything but a spinster." Edward Nehls, ed., *D. H. Lawrence: A Composite Biography* (Madison, 1957), II, 412.

67. Although Sinclair admired Lawrence's works, she had reservations about Lawrence as a person according to an account given by Hilda Doolittle in *Bid me to Live: A Madrigal* (New York, 1960), pp. 168 - 69. In this autobiographical novel, "H. D." recalls that May Sinclair, who appears in the novel as the character Miss Kerr, advised her not to get involved with the Lawrences. As Sinclair had foreseen, "H. D.'s" experience with Lawrence proved traumatic. But, according to "H. D.," Sinclair, in spite of her warning, had succumbed to Lawrence's charm, relating to "H. D." that Lawrence had told her that the name of the tree in her garden, which no one before had been able to identify, was "Key-of-Heaven tree." The name apparently caught Sinclair's imagination, for she used it as a title to a subsequent novel, *The Tree of Heaven*.

68. Edward Nehls, ed., *D. H. Lawrence: A Composite Biography*, I, 579.

69. D. H. Lawrence, *Letters*, ed. Aldous Huxley (New York, 1932), p. 368.

70. Emile Delavenay, *D. H. Lawrence: The Man and His Work* (London, 1972), p. 107.

71. Ibid., pp. 263, 310, 361, 519.

72. Curtis Brown, *Contacts* (New York, 1935), p. 168.

73. *The Three Sisters*, p. 1.

74. Ibid., pp. 184 - 85.

75. Ibid., p. 369.

76. Ibid., p. 161.

77. Boll, "May Sinclair and the Medico-Psychological Clinic of London," p. 315.

78. Sinclair to Richard W. Gilder, April 7, 1909, University of Texas Library.

79. Sinclair to Richard Gilder, June 13, 1909, and June 25, 1909, University of Texas Library.

80. Dixon, p. 123.

81. Sinclair to Thomas Hardy, July 9, 1909, Dorset County Museum, Thomas Hardy Collection.

82. *The Three Brontës*, p. 123.

83. *The Three Sisters*, p. 132.

84. Pound, *Letters*, p. 46.

Chapter Five

1. Wyndham Lewis, *Blasting and Bombardiering* (London, 1967), p. 223.

2. Marie Belloc-Loundes, *A Passing World* (London, 1948), p. 196.

3. *A Journal of Impressions in Belgium* (London, 1915), p. 17.

4. Ibid., p. 194.

5. Belloc-Loundes, p. 197.

6. *A Journal*, p. 249.

7. Ibid., p. v.

8. Ibid., p. 259.

9. Ibid., p. 305.

10. May Sinclair to Bertrand Russell, February 29, 1918, The Bertrand Russell Archives, Mills Memorial Library, McMaster University.

11. *Manchester Guardian*, November 13, 1914, p. 7.

12. "Worse than War," *English Review* 31 (August, 1920), 153.

13. Arnold Bennett, *Journals of Arnold Bennett*, ed. Newman Flower, 3 vols. (London, 1932 - 1933), II, 7.

14. Arnold Bennett, "Books and Persons," *The New Age* 3 (August 8, 1908), 293.

15. Arnold Bennett, "Books and Persons," *The New Age* 4 (February 11, 1909), 325.

16. Arnold Bennett, "Books and Persons," *The New Age* 4 (February 4, 1909), 305.

17. Bennett, *Journals of Arnold Bennett, 1921 - 1928*, III, 245.

18. Willis Steele, p. 559.

19. Alice Payne Hackett, *Sixty Years of Best Sellers 1895 - 1955* (New York, 1956), p. 124.

20. *The Tree of Heaven*, (New York, 1918), p. 392.

21. Ibid., p. 396.

22. Ibid.

23. Ibid., p. 397.

24. Ibid., p. 241.

25. Ibid., p. 243.

26. Ibid., p. 185.

27. See Glenn S. Burne, *Rémy de Gourmont, his Ideas and Influence in England and America* (Carbondale, Ill., 1963).

28. Some of the violent quarrels that periodically broke out among this

group of artists and writers are related by William C. Wees in *Vorticism and the English Avant-Garde* (Manchester, 1972), pp. 46, 72.

29. Lawrence Gilman, "May Sinclair's New War Novel," *North American Review* 207 (February, 1918), 284.

30. See *The Tree of Heaven*, pp. 372, 395.

31. Lewis, p. 35.

32. Anon., "The Tree of Heaven," *Times Literary Supplement*, October 25, 1917, p. 516.

33. Sinclair to George P. Brett, October 24, 1919, Macmillan Collection, New York Public Library.

34. R. Walker, p. 2.

Chapter Six

1. "On Imagism," *The Egoist* 2 (June, 1915), 88 - 89.

2. Wallace Martin, "Sources of the Imagist Aesthetic," *Publications of the Modern Language Association* 85 (March, 1970), 201 - 4. See also William Pratt, *The Imagist Poem: Modern Poetry in Miniature* (New York, 1963), pp. 34 - 35.

3. "The Poems of F. S. Flint," *English Review* 32 (January, 1921), 7.

4. T. E. Hulme, "A Lecture on Modern Poetry," in *Further Speculations*, ed. Samuel Hynes (St. Paul, Minn., 1955), p. 72.

5. F. S. Flint, "Imagisme," *Poetry* 1 (March, 1913), 199.

6. "The Poems of F. S. Flint," p. 5.

7. Joseph Warren Beach, *The Twentieth-Century Novel: Studies in Technique* (New York, 1932), pp. 385 - 86.

8. Randolph Bourne, "An Imagist Novel," *The Dial* 64 (May, 1918), 451.

9. "The Novels of Dorothy Richardson," *The Egoist* 5 (April, 1918), 59.

10. Hulme, p. 68.

11. "Dorothy Richardson," p. 58.

12. Ibid., p. 57.

13. Walter Allen, "Introduction," in *Pilgrimmage*, p. 5.

14. Virginia Woolf, "Modern Fiction," in *The Common Reader* (New York, 1925), p. 212.

15. As quoted by J. Isaacs, *An Assessment of Twentieth-Century Literature* (London, 1951), p. 88.

16. "Dorothy Richardson," p. 58.

17. Virginia Woolf, "Modern Fiction," p. 212.

18. Ibid., p. 211.

19. "Dorothy Richardson," p. 57.

20. Laura Martin Jarman, "The Goncourt Brothers; Modernists in Abnormal Psychology," *University of New Mexico Bulletin* 6, no. 3 (April, 1939), 37 - 40.

21. *Mary Olivier: A Life* (New York, 1919), p. 113.

22. Ibid., p. 141.

23. Ibid., p. 294.

24. Ibid., pp. 290 - 91.

25. Ibid., p. 314.

26. Ibid., pp. 310 - 13.

27. Ibid., p. 170.

28. Ibid., p. 194.

29. Ibid., p. 251.

30. Anon., "A Psychoanalytic Interpretation of a Life," *New York Medical Journal* 20 (March 6, 1920), 430.

31. *Mary Olivier*, p. 320.

32. Evelyn Underhill, *Mysticism* (New York, 1961), p. xv.

33. *Mary Olivier*, p. 93.

34. Underhill, p. 197.

35. Ibid., p. 177.

36. Ibid., p. 196.

37. Ibid., p. 211.

38. Ibid., p. 221.

39. Ibid., p. 205.

40. Ibid., p. 234.

41. *Mary Olivier*, p. 269.

42. Ibid., p. 375.

43. Sinclair to H. G. Wells, October 16, 1915, University of Illinois Library, Urbana.

44. *Mary Olivier*, pp. 58 - 59.

45. Ibid., p. 226.

46. Anon., "Mary Olivier," *Times Literary Supplement,* June 12, 1919, p. 324.

47. Sinclair to H. G. Wells, June 29, 1919, University of Illinois Library, Urbana.

48. Katherine Mansfield, *Novels and Novelists* (London, 1930), p. 41.

49. Ibid., p. 42.

50. Richard Aldington, *Literary Studies and Reviews* (London, 1924), pp. 178 - 79.

51. E. M. Forster, "A Moving Document," *Daily Herald,* July 30, 1919, p. 8.

52. Ibid.

53. Ibid.

54. Frierson, pp. 190 - 92.

55. *Pilgrimage*, II, 222.

56. Gloria Glikin, "Dorothy Richardson: The Personal 'Pilgrimage,'" *Publications of the Modern Language Association* 88 (December, 1963), 586 - 600.

57. Dorothy Richardson, *Pilgrimage — Honeycomb* (New York, 1917), p. 252.

58. Richardson, *Pilgrimage,* II, 136.

59. Ibid., III, 246.
60. Ibid., p. 247.
61. Ibid., IV, 658.
62. Ibid., III, 503.
63. Ibid., IV, 607.
64. Ibid., p. 155.
65. Babette Deutsch, "Freedom and the Grace of God," *The Dial* 67 (November 15, 1919), 442.
66. Caesar R. Blake, *Dorothy Richardson* (Ann Arbor, 1960), p. 190.
67. Ibid.
68. Richardson, *Pilgrimage*, IV, 657.
69. *Mary Olivier*, p. 378.
70. Shiv K. Kumar, *Bergson and the Stream of Consciousness Novel* (New York, 1963), p. 39.
71. Blake, p. 196.
72. According to the *Report of the Royal Commission on the Care and Control of the Feeble-Minded*, published in 1908, mental defectiveness, including mental illness, was caused by heredity. Samuel Hynes, *The Edwardian Turn of Mind*, pp. 32 - 33.

Chapter Seven

1. *Life and Death of Harriett Frean* (New York, 1922), p. 15; originally published in 1920.
2. Ibid., pp. 19 - 20.
3. Ibid., p. 81.
4. Ibid., p. 82.
5. Ibid., p. 117.
6. Ibid., p. 100.
7. Ibid., p. 131.
8. Ibid., pp. 132 - 33.
9. Virginia Woolf and Lytton Strachey, *Letters*, ed. Leonard Woolf and James Strachey (New York, 1956), p. 139. The conclusion in *Queen Victoria* (1921) echoes the conclusion in *Harriett Frean*. Strachey concludes with a narrative of Queen Victoria's thoughts "in the secret chambers of her consciousness" as she is dying, in which she proceeds to older and older memories until like Harriett, who thinks of herself as an infant in her crib with her mother standing by, Queen Victoria thinks of herself as an infant on a rug with her mother sweeping toward her. One wonders if Strachey read Sinclair's novel when it was being serialized in the *North American Review* from December, 1920, to March, 1921.
10. Sinclair to Sinclair Lewis, January 25, 1922, Yale University Library.
11. Virginia Woolf, *A Writer's Diary* (London, 1953), p. 23.
12. "The Future of the Novel," *Pall Mall Gazette*, January 10, 1921, p. 7.
13. *Harriett Frean*, p. 51.

14. Ibid., p. 123.

15. Robert Humphrey, *Stream of Consciousness in the Modern Novel* (Berkeley, 1965), p. 34.

16. Dan Jacobson, "Muffled Majesty," *Times Literary Supplement*, October 26, 1967, p. 1007. For the *locus classicus* of the problems of impersonal narration, see Part III of Wayne C. Booth's *The Rhetoric of Fiction* (Chicago, 1961).

17. Anon., "Psychoanalysis," *Pall Mall Gazette*, January 5, 1921, p. 6.

18. Anon., "A Mother Complex," *Times Literary Supplement*, February 2, 1922, p. 73.

19. T. S. Eliot, "London Letter," *The Dial* 73 (September, 1922), 330.

20. J. D. Beresford, "Le Décline de l'Influence de la Psycho-Analyse sur le Roman Anglais," *Mercure de France* 190 (September, 1926), 263 (my translation).

21. Una Hunt, "Life and Death of Harriett Frean," *The New Republic* 31 (July, 1922), 260.

22. T. S. Eliot, "London Letter."

23. Sinclair to Mr. Maas, August 30, 1921, The Bancroft Library, University of California, Berkeley.

24. Sinclair to Hugh Walpole, March 4, 1916, University of Texas Library.

25. Sinclair to Hugh Walpole, April 27, 1919, University of Texas Library.

26. Sinclair to Violet Hunt, December 16, 1922, Berg Collection, New York Public Library.

27. *Defence of Idealism*, p. 248.

28. Annis Pratt, "Women and Nature in Modern Fiction," *Contemporary Literature* 13, no. 4 (1972), 484.

Chapter Eight

1. *Mr. Waddington of Wyck* (New York, 1921), p. 302.

2. Ibid., p. 306.

3. Ibid., p. 209.

4. Ibid., p. 313.

5. *A Cure of Souls* (New York, 1924), p. 54.

6. Ibid., p. 56.

7. Ibid., pp. 58 - 59.

8. Ibid., p. 62.

9. Ibid., p. 89.

10. Ibid., p. 60.

11. Ibid., p. 2.

12. Anon., "May Sinclair," *The Times*, November 15, 1946, p. 7e.

13. Martin Armstrong, "The Pagan in the Parsonage," *Spectator* 132 (March 22, 1924), 466.

14. Anon., "Topics of the Times, What Grievance Have These Novelists?" *New York Times*, February 1, 1924, p. 16f.

15. Joseph Wood Krutch, "From Wisdom's Mountain Height," *The Nation* (May 7, 1924), p. 536.

16. "Jones's Karma," *Criterion* 2 (October, 1923), 56.

17. Herbert Howarth, *Notes on Some Figures Behind T. S. Eliot* (Boston, 1964), pp. 272 - 77.

18. Sinclair to John Cournos, August 30, 1921, Fales Collection, New York University Library.

19. Sinclair to T. S. Eliot, May 15, 1922, Harvard University Library.

20. "The Child," *The Egoist* 4 (February, 1917), 24, and "Numbers," *The Egoist* 5 (October, 1918), 122 - 23.

21. Sinclair to Charlotte Mary Mew, June 9, 1915, Berg Collection, New York Public Library.

22. Sinclair to Mrs. Glover, May 14, 1917, University of Texas Library.

Chapter Nine

1. Paul West, *The Modern Novel* (London, 1963), I, 76.

2. May Sinclair to Bertrand Russell, September 21, 1917, and June 7, 1919, Bertrand Russell Archives, Mills Memorial Library, McMaster University.

3. May Sinclair to Edward Garnett, March 12, 1902? University of Texas Library.

4. C. A. Dawson Scott, "Miss May Sinclair," *The Bookman* 59 (October, 1920), 7 - 9.

5. L. P. Hartley, "New Fiction [a review of *Anthony Waring*]," *Saturday Review* 144 (September 17, 1927), 370.

6. Horace Gregory, "May Sinclair Vivisects Some Pre-War People," *New York Evening Post*, September 20, 1930, p. 12.

Selected Bibliography

BIBLIOGRAPHY

Boll, T. E. M. "May Sinclair: A Check List." *Bulletin of the New York Public Library* 74 (September, 1970), 459 - 67. Lists uncollected short stories, poems, book reviews, articles for the *Cheltenham Ladies College Magazine*, and letters to the editor.

PRIMARY SOURCES

1. Novels

Audrey Craven. London: Blackwood & Son, 1897; New York: Henry Holt, 1906.

Mr. and Mrs. Nevill Tyson. London: Blackwood & Son, 1898. Published in America as *The Tysons*. New York: B. W. Dodge, 1906.

Two Sides of a Question. [*The Cosmopolitan* and *Superseded*] London: Constable, 1901; New York: J. F. Taylor & Co., 1901. Two novellas.

The Divine Fire. London: Constable, 1904; New York: Henry Holt, 1904.

The Helpmate. London: Constable, 1907; New York: Henry Holt, 1907. Serialized in *Atlantic Monthly*, (January - September, 1907).

The Judgment of Eve. New York: Harper, 1908. London: supplement to *The Lady's Realm*, December, 1907.

Kitty Tailleur. London: Constable, 1908. Published in America as *The Immortal Moment: The Story of Kitty Tailleur*. New York: Doubleday, 1908.

The Creators: A Comedy. London: Constable, 1910; New York: Century Co., 1910. Serialized in *Century Magazine* (November, 1909 - December, 1910).

The Flaw in the Crystal. New York: Dutton, 1912. *English Review* (September, 1912).

The Combined Maze. London: Hutchinson, 1913; New York: Harper, 1913.

The Three Sisters. London: Hutchinson, 1914; New York: Macmillan, 1914.

Tasker Jevons: The Real Story. London: Hutchinson, 1916. Published in America as *The Belfry*. New York: Macmillan, 1916.

The Tree of Heaven. London: Cassell, 1917; New York: Macmillan, 1917.
Mary Olivier: A Life. London: Cassell, 1919; New York: Macmillan, 1919.
    Serialized in *The Little Review* (January - May, 1919).
The Romantic. London: Collins, 1920; New York: Macmillan, 1920.
Mr. Waddington of Wyck. London: Cassell, 1921; New York: Macmillan, 1921.
Life and Death of Harriett Frean. London: Collins, 1922; New York: Macmillan, 1922. Serialized in *North American Review* (December 1920 - March 1921).
Anne Severn and the Fieldings. London: Hutchinson, 1922; New York: Macmillan, 1922.
A Cure of Souls. London: Hutchinson, 1924; New York: Macmillan, 1924.
The Dark Night: A Novel in Verse. London: Cape, 1924; New York: Macmillan, 1924.
Arnold Waterlow: A Life. London: Hutchinson, 1924; New York: Macmillan, 1924.
The Rector of Wyck. London: Hutchinson, 1925; New York: Macmillan, 1925.
Far End. London: Hutchinson, 1926; New York: Macmillan, 1926.
The Allinghams. London: Hutchinson, 1927; New York: Macmillan, 1927.
History of Anthony Waring. London: Hutchinson, 1927; New York: Macmillan, 1927.

2. Collections of Short Stories

The Judgment of Eve and Other Stories. London: Hutchinson, 1914.
The Return of the Prodigal and Other Stories. New York: Macmillan, 1914.
    (Includes *The Cosmopolitan;* omits *The Judgment of Eve;* otherwise contents the same as the previous book.)
Uncanny Stories. London: Hutchinson, 1923; New York: Macmillan, 1923.
Tales Told by Simpson. London: Hutchinson, 1930; New York: Macmillan, 1930.
The Intercessor and Other Stories. London: Hutchinson, 1931; New York: Macmillan, 1932.

3. Verse

Nakiketas and Other Poems. [by Julian Sinclair.] London: Kegan Paul, 1886.
Essays in Verse. London: Kegan Paul, 1892.

4. Works on Philosophy and Psychology

"The Ethical and Religious Import of Idealism." *The New World* 2 (December, 1893), 694 - 708.
"Symbolism and Sublimation I." *Medical Press and Circular* 153 (August 9, 1916), 118 - 22.
"Symbolism and Sublimation II." *Medical Press and Circular* 153 (August 16, 1916), 142 - 45.

A Defence of Idealism: Some Questions and Conclusions. London: Macmillan, 1917; New York: Macmillan, 1917.

The New Idealism. London: Macmillan, 1922; New York, Macmillan, 1922.

"Psychological Types." *English Review* 36 (May, 1923), 436 - 39. Review of Jung's *Psychological Types.*

"Primary and Secondary Consciousness." *Proceedings of the Aristotelian Society*, n.s. 23 (1923), 111 - 20.

5. Works on the Brontës

Introductions to the Brontë Everyman Series published by Dent, London:
  Wuthering Heights by Emily Brontë. 1907. pp. vii - xiii.
  Jane Eyre by Charlotte Brontë. 1908. pp. vii - xvii.
  The Life of Charlotte Brontë by E. C. Gaskell. 1908. pp. vii - xxii.
  Shirley by Charlotte Brontë. 1908. pp. vii - xv.
  Villette by Charlotte Brontë. 1909. pp. vii - xv.
  The Professor by Charlotte Brontë. 1910. pp. vii - xi.
  The Tenant of Wildfell Hall by Anne Brontë. 1914. pp. vii - xiii.
The Three Brontës. London: Hutchinson, 1912; New York: Houghton Mifflin, 1912.

"The New Brontë Letters." *The Dial* 60 (November, 1913), 343 - 46.

6. Articles on Other Literary Subjects

"Man and Superman: A Symposium." *New York Times*, Holiday Book Number, Literary Section, December 1, 1905, pp. 813 - 14. On Shaw's play.

"Three American Poets of Today: Edward Arlington Robinson, William Vaughan Moody and Ridgely Torrence." *Atlantic Monthly* 98 (September, 1906), 325 - 35.

"The Novels of George Meredith." *Outlook* 92 (June, 1909), 413 - 18.

"The Gitanjali: or Song Offerings of Rabindra Nath Tagore." *North American Review* 197 (May, 1913), 659 - 76.

"Two Notes" I "On H. D." II "On Imagism." *The Egoist* 2 (June, 1915), 88 - 89.

"Introduction." In *The Closed Door* by Jean de Bosschère. London: John Lane, 1917.

"Prufrock: and Other Observations." *The Little Review* 4 (December, 1917), 8 - 14.

"The Novels of Dorothy Richardson." *The Egoist* 5 (April, 1918), 57 - 59. *The Little Review* 5 (April, 1918), 3 - 11. Reprinted as "Introduction" to *Pilgrimage* by Dorothy Richardson. New York: Knopf, 1919.

"The Reputation of Ezra Pound." *English Review* 30 (April, 1920), 326 - 35. *North American Review* 211 (May, 1920), 658 - 68.

"The Poems of F. S. Flint." *English Review* 32 (January, 1921), 6 - 18.

"The Future of the Novel." *Pall Mall Gazette*, January 10, 1921, p. 7.

"The Poems of Richard Aldington." *English Review* 32 (May, 1921), 397 - 410.

"The Novels of Violet Hunt." *English Review* 34 (February, 1922), 106 - 18.
"The Poems of H. D." *The Dial* 72 (February, 1922), 203 - 7.
"The Man From Main Street." *New York Times Book Review*, September 24, 1922, p. 1. Review of *Babbitt* by Sinclair Lewis.

7. Miscellaneous Works (World War I and Feminism)

Feminism. The Women Writers Suffrage League. London, 1912. A pamphlet. "A Defence of Men." *English Review* 10 (July, 1912), 556 - 566; *Forum* 48 (October, 1912), 409 - 20.
America's Part in the War. The Committee for Relief in Belgium — The Woman's Section. New York: April, 1915. A pamphlet.
A Journal of Impressions in Belgium. London: Hutchinson, 1915; New York: Macmillan, 1915.
"Worse than War." *English Review* 31 (August, 1920), 147 - 53.

8. Translations

Rudolf Sohm. *Outlines of Church History*. London: Macmillan, 1895; Boston: Beacon Press, 1958.
Theodore von Sosnosky. *England's Danger, The Future of British Army Reform*. London: Chapman & Hall, 1901.

SECONDARY SOURCES

ALDINGTON, RICHARD. *Life for Life's Sake*. New York: Viking Press, 1941. Few brief references to Sinclair.
ALLEN, WALTER. *The Modern Novel: in Britain and in the United States*. New York: E. P. Dutton, 1964. Praises *Mary Olivier* and *Harriett Frean*, "her masterpiece."
————. "Introduction." In *Pilgrimage* by Dorothy Richardson. Vol. I. New York: Knopf, 1967. Sinclair's review "a classic of modern criticism of fiction."
BEACH, JOSEPH WARREN. *English Literature of the Nineteenth and Early Twentieth Centuries*. New York: Collier, 1962. Her works merit further study.
BELLOC-LOWNDES, MARIE. *A Passing World*. London: Macmillan, 1948. Biographical facts and speculations about Sinclair.
BENNETT, ARNOLD. "Books and Persons." *The New Age* 4 (February 11, 1909), 325. Includes Sinclair with writers who cater to the tastes of the middle class.
————. *Journals of Arnold Bennett*, ed. Newman Flower. Vol. II: *1911 - 1921*. Vol. III: *1921 - 1928*. London: Cassel & Co., 1932 - 1933. Recounts two meetings with Sinclair.
BOLL, THEOPHILUS E. M. "*The Divine Fire* (1904) and *Martin Eden* (1909)," *English Literature in Transition* 14, no. 2 (1971), 115 - 17. Jack London indebted to Sinclair's novel.
————. "May Sinclair and the Medico-Psychological Clinic of London."

Proceedings of the American Philosophical Society 106 (August, 1962), 310 - 26. History of the Clinic and Sinclair's connection with it. Interesting and thorough research.

————. *Miss May Sinclair: Novelist.* Rutherford, N.J.: Fairleigh Dickinson University Press, 1973. A wealth of material about Sinclair's life and works, but tends to be hagiographic rather than discriminating.

————. "The Mystery of Charlotte Mew and May Sinclair: An Inquiry." *Bulletin of the New York Public Library* 74 (September, 1970), 445 - 53. Sinclair repulsed Mew's lesbian advances.

————. "On the May Sinclair Collection." *Library Chronicle.* 27 (1961), 1 - 15. Description of the Sinclair papers Dr. Boll secured from the Sinclair family for the University of Pennsylvania library.

BOSSCHÈRE, JEAN DE. "Charity in the Work of May Sinclair." *Yale Review* 14 (October, 1924), 82 - 94. Appreciative but not analytical article by Sinclair's friend.

BRAYBROOKE, PATRICK. *Novelists We Are Seven.* Philadelphia: J. P. Lippincott Co., 1926. Twenty pages on Sinclair; her novels profoundly introspective, deep and intelligent but "she knows too much."

BREWSTER, DOROTHY, and BIRRELL, ANGUS. *Dead Reckonings in Fiction.* New York: Longmans, 1924. Fifty pages on Sinclair's novels. Interesting comparisons between Sinclair's novels and those of George Eliot, Hardy, and Lawrence. Slightly shorter version in their *Modern Fiction.* New York: Columbia University Press, 1934.

BULLETT, GERALD. *Modern English Fiction.* London: Herbert Jenkins, 1926. Refers to her sense of dramatic values, vivid and economical narrative, wit and irony.

CHEVALLEY, ABEL. *The Modern English Novel.* New York: Knopf, 1921. Ten pages of favorable comments on Sinclair's novels.

COOPER, FREDERIC T. *Some English Story Tellers.* London: Grant Richards, 1912. Almost thirty pages on Sinclair's early novels.

DEUTSCH, BABETTE. "Freedom and the Grace of God." *The Dial* 77 (November 15, 1919), 441 - 42. Finds echoes of Sinclair's *Defence of Idealism* in Dorothy Richardson's *Tunnel.*

DREW, ELIZABETH. *The Modern Novel: Some Aspects of Contemporary Fiction.* London: Jonathan Cape, 1926. Many references in passing to Sinclair's novels.

DRINKWATER, JOHN. *The Outline of Literature.* London: George Newnes, 1950. Sinclair's literary criticism original and distinctive; deserves to be better known.

ELIOT, T. S. "London Letter." *The Dial* 73 (September, 1922), 330 - 31. Praises *Harriett Frean*, but Sinclair has carried the psychoanalytic method in literature as far as it can go.

ELWIN, MALCOLM. *Old Gods Falling.* London: Collins, 1939. Sinclair shows sensitive understanding of passion; combines the different genius of Charlotte and Emily Brontë.

FORD, FORD MADOX. "Literary Portraits VI, Miss May Sinclair." *The*

Tribune, August 31, 1907, p. 2. Criticism of *The Divine Fire* and *The Helpmate*.

————. "Literary Portraits XXXIV, Miss May Sinclair and 'The Judgment of Eve.' " *Outlook*, May 2, 1914, pp. 599 - 600. Sinclair was practicing a greater intensity and a more concentrated form.

————. *Return to Yesterday: Reminiscenses, 1894 - 1914.* London: Gollanz, 1931. Some anecdotes about Sinclair.

FORSTER, E. M. "A Moving Document." *Daily Herald*, July 30, 1919, p. 8. Favorable review of *Mary Olivier*.

FRIERSON, W. C. *The English Novel in Transition.* Norman: University of Oklahoma Press, 1942. Emphasizes her naturalistic vision and her revolt against Victorian values.

FROST, ROBERT. *Selected Letters.* edited by Lawrence Thompson. New York: Holt, Rinehart and Winston, 1963. Refers to Sinclair's attempts to make his poems known in England.

GORSKY, SUSAN. "The Gentle Doubters: Images of Women in English-women's Novels, 1840 - 1920." *Images of Women in Fiction: Feminine Perspectives*, edited by Susan Koppelman Cornillon, pp. 28 - 54. Bowling Green: Bowling Green University Press, 1972. Sinclair probes into role of women in *The Creators* and *The Helpmate*.

GOULD, GERALD. *The English Novel of To-Day.* London: John Castle, 1924. About twelve pages on Sinclair's novels.

H. D. [HILDA DOOLITTLE]. *Bid Me to Live: A Madrigal.* New York: Grove Press, 1960. Autobiographical *román a clef* in which "Miss Kerr," May Sinclair, warns H. D. not to become involved with the Lawrences.

HOOPS, REINALD. *Der Einfluss der Psychoanalyse auf die Englische Literatur.* Heidelberg: C. Winter, 1934. Sees some psychoanalytic themes in Sinclair's early novels.

HOWARTH, HERBERT. *Notes on Some Figures Behind T. S. Eliot.* Boston: Houghton Mifflin, 1964. Fives pages on Sinclair's influence on Eliot.

JOHNSON, R. BRIMLEY. *Some Contemporary Novelists (Women).* London: Leonard Parsons, 1920. Ten pages on Sinclair's novels.

KAPLAN, SYDNEY. "Featureless Freedom or Ironic Submission: Dorothy Richardson and May Sinclair." *College English* 32 (May, 1971), 914 - 17. Comparison between *Mary Olivier* and *Pilgrimage*. Sinclair more deterministic and her heroine more submissive.

————. *Feminine Consciousness in the Modern British Novel.* Urbana: University of Illinois Press, 1975. Thirty pages on *Mary Olivier*. Analyzes style of Mary Olivier's stream of consciousness and emphasizes Sinclair's determinism.

KUMAR, SHIV K. *Bergson and the Stream of Consciousness Novel.* New York: New York University Press, 1963. Dorothy Richardson's interest in idealistic philosophy may have been aroused through Sinclair's book on idealism.

KUNITZ, STANLEY J., and HAYCRAFT, HOWARD, eds. *Twentieth Century Authors*. New York: H. W. Wilson Company, 1942. Brief life.

LAWRENCE, D. H. *Letters*. Edited by Aldous Huxley. New York: Viking Press, 1932. Refers to *The Three Sisters*.

MANSFIELD, KATHERINE. *Novels and Novelists*. London: Constable, 1930. Unfavorable review of *Mary Olivier*.

MYERS, WALTER. *The Later Realism: A Study of Characterization in the British Novel*. Chicago: University of Chicago Press, 1924. About ten pages of sympathetic discussion of Sinclair's novels.

PHELPS, WILLIAM LYON. *The Advance of the English Novel*. New York: Dodd Mead, 1916. Refers to Sinclair's high reputation at the time.

PRATT, ANNIS. "Women and Nature in Modern Fiction." *Contemporary Literature* 13, no. 4 (1972), 476 - 91. Mary Olivier gives up her lover because she is more devoted to her "psychic development in naturism" and to her life as a writer; social expectations in marriage would threaten her identity.

RAIKES, ELIZABETH. *Dorothea Beale of Cheltenham*. London: Constable, 1908. Five pages of extracts from the correspondence between "a former student," actually Sinclair, and Miss Beale showing Sinclair's relative poverty in the 1880s and 1890s and her religious questioning.

ROBB, KENNETH A. "May Sinclair: An Annotated Bibliography of Writings About Her." *English Literature in Transition* 16, no. 3 (1973), 177 - 231. Very thorough.

STEELL, WILLIS. "May Sinclair Tells Why She Isn't a Poet." *Literary Digest International Book Review* 2 (June, 1924), 513, 559. Biographical details about her childhood.

STEVENSON, LIONEL. *The History of the English Novel. Yesterday and After*. Vol. XI. New York: Barnes and Noble, 1967. In a chapter entitled "A Group of Able Dames," Stevenson gives a seven-page mixed review of Sinclair's novels.

SWINNERTON, FRANK. *The Georgian Scene: A Literary Panorama*. New York: Farrar & Rinehart, 1934. Sinclair took interesting steps in the novel.

TAYLOR, CORRINE Y. "A Study of May Sinclair — Woman and Writer, 1863 - 1946 — with an Annotated Bibliography." Ph.D. dissertation, Washington State University, 1969. Consists mostly of summaries of reviews of each of Sinclair's works received at the time of publication. No analysis of novels.

TYNAN, KATHARINE. *The Middle Years*. London: Constable, 1916. Biographical details about Sinclair's early years as a writer.

WAGENKNECHT, EDWARD. *Cavalcade of the English Novel*. New York: Henry Holt, 1943. Sinclair interested in the family group and relationship of individual to it.

WALKER, R. "May Sinclair Talks of Everything Except Herself." *New York Times Book Review*, May 18, 1924, p. 2. Sinclair lists her favorites among modern novelists and poets; gives her views on politics and on the modern novel.

WEST, PAUL. *The Modern Novel: England and France.* 2 vols. London: Hutchinson, 1963. A two-page review of Sinclair's major novels. Finds them too analytical; subject matter too obtrusively that of abnormal psychology.

ZEGGER, HRISEY DIMITRAKIS. "May Sinclair's Psychological Novels." Ph.D. dissertation, New York University, 1970. Analysis of the major novels.

Index

Goldring, Douglas, 27
Goncourt, Jules and Edmond, 99
Gourmont, Rémy de, 92
Green, T. H., 17, 19 - 22, 107, 116

Haeckel, Ernst, 104
Hard Times (Dickens), 21
Hardy, Thomas, 24, 49, 54, 65, 66, 78, 80
Hartley, L. P., 146
H. D. (Hilda Doolittle), 24, 158n67
Hegel, Georg, 16, 104
Hobhouse, L. T., 22
Hulme, T. E., 96
Hunt, Violet, 24
Hysteria, 70, 118

Ibsen, Henrik, 40
Idealism, 17, 19 - 22, 29, 30 - 31, 37, 39,
    41, 52, 59, 107, 109, 115, 116, 128,
    139, 140, 144
Imagism, 24, 25, 26, 92, 93, 95 - 98, 101
Insanity, 114, 118
Irony, 38 - 39, 138

James, Henry, 20, 21, 24, 32, 48, 60 - 65,
    67, 87, 95, 129, 153n20
James, William, 98, 151n42
Janet, Pierre, 22, 57, 70
Jean Christophe (Rolland), 113
Joad, C. E. M., 19
Jones, Lawrence, 22, 42, 73
Joyce, James, 25, 99, 124, 126
Jung, Carl, 22, 58, 59, 64, 80

Kant, Immanuel, 16
Kingsley, Charles, 40, 42

Lady Chatterly's Lover (Lawrence), 75
Lawrence, D. H., 17, 46, 65, 73 - 78,
    158n66, 158n67
Lessing, Doris, 146
Lewis, Sinclair, 23
Lewis, Wyndham, 25, 27, 82, 92, 93,
    152n71
London, Jack, 36
London Library, 16

Macmillan's Magazine, 18
McTaggart, J. M. E., 21, 115
Man and Superman (Shaw), 47

Manchester Guardian, 84
Mansfield, Katherine, 111
Marianne Thornton (E. M. Forster), 91
Marriage, 40, 41, 45, 52, 53 - 55, 56
Marriage (Wells), 53
Medico-Psychological Clinic, 22, 58, 80
Mental State of Hystericals (Janet), 57
Meredith, George, 43
Mew, Charlotte Mary, 25
Monroe, Harriet, 23
Moore, George, 156n18
Moore, G. E., 18, 116
Motor Field Ambulance Corps, 82, 84
Muirhead, J. H., 21
Munro, Hector, 80, 82 - 83
Mysticism, 105, 107 - 10, 115, 118, 131,
    134

Naturalism, 40, 41, 51, 52, 95, 99, 144
New Freewoman, 24
New Grub Street (Gissing), 36
New Machiavelli, The (Wells), 53, 55
New psychology, 126. See also psycho-
    analysis
New Statesman, 25
New woman, 110, 130
New York City, 23, 27
Nicoll, William Robertson, 87
Nightingale, Florence, 72
Novel of ideas, 42, 50

Orwell, George, 26

Patmore, Coventry, 40
P. E. N., 27, 88
Pilgrimage (Richardson), 96, 97 - 99,
    114 - 15, 117, 124, 126, 145
Portrait of a Lady (James), 21, 65
Pound, Ezra, 17, 23, 24 - 25, 26, 81, 91,
    96
Proceedings of the Society for Psychical
    Research, 57
Professor, The (Brontë), 67, 80
Psychoanalysis, 22, 26, 57 - 59, 63, 68,
    71, 77, 80, 101, 106, 109, 123, 127,
    130, 143, 144, 145

Quarterly Review, 25

Rainbow, The (Lawrence), 74, 77
Realism, 36, 39 - 30, 57, 60, 115